In the Name of Tradition

Female Genital Mutilation in Iran

Kameel Ahmady

In the Name of Tradition

Female Genital Mutilation in Iran

AfterWords

by Tobe Levin and Hilary Burrage

UnCUT/VOICES Press
2016

ISBN: 978-3-9813863-7-0

Bibliographic information published by the Deutsche Nationalbibliothek. The Deutsche Nationalbibliothek lists this publication in the Deutsche Nationalbibliografie; detailed bibliographic data are available on the Internet at http://dnb.d-nb.de
Frankfurt am Main: UnCUT/VOICES Press, 2016.

The cover pastel by Godfrey Williams-Okorodus is titled "In Our Hands." All charts and graphs © Kameel Ahmady

About UnCUT/VOICES Press ...

Founded in Frankfurt am Main, Germany, UnCUT/VOICES Press is the first publisher to focus solely on female genital mutilation. By translating studies of FGM from French, German and other languages, UnCUT/VOICES Press broadens access to these indispensable resources. It also features significant and rare material in English aimed at ending an egregious injury still inflicted on girls.

The founder Tobe Levin von Gleichen, a Visiting Research Fellow in International Gender Studies at Lady Margaret Hall, University of Oxford and an Associate of the Hutchins Center for African and African American Research at Harvard University, has been active against FGM since 1977. Co-editor with Augustine H. Asaah of *Empathy and Rage. Female Genital Mutilation in African Literature* (Ayebia, 2009), she served as founding president of FORWARD-Germany and has advised the Austrian Parliament, the Bundestag, Westminster, UNICEF and WHO. See also Levin, Tobe, ed. *Waging Empathy. Alice Walker, Possessing the Secret of Joy and the Global Movement to Ban FGM*. Frankfurt am Main: UnCUT/VOICES Press, 2014.

UnCUT/VOICES PRESS
Martin Luther Str. 35, 60389 Frankfurt am Main, Germany
Tobe.levin@uncutvoices.com www.uncutvoices.wordpress.com
Geschäftsnummer HRB 86527, U.G. Haftungsbeschränkt

Also from UnCUT/VOICES Press

Khady with Marie-Thérèse Cuny. *Blood Stains. A Child of Africa Reclaims her Human Rights*. Trans. Tobe Levin. Frankfurt am Main: UnCUT/VOICES Press, 2010.

Prolongeau, Hubert. *Undoing FGM. Pierre Foldes, the Surgeon Who Restores the Clitoris*. Foreword Bernard Kouchner. Trans. and Afterword Tobe Levin. Frankfurt am Main: UnCUT/VOICES Press, 2011.

Mwaluko, Nick Hadikwa. *WAAFRIKA. 1992. Kenya. Two Women Fall in Love*. Frankfurt am Main: UnCUT/VOICES Press, 2013.

Hutton, Frankie, ed. *Rose Lore. Essays in Cultural History and Semiotics*. Frankfurt am Main: UnCUT/VOICES Press, 2015. With a chapter on FGM by Tobe Levin.

Kiminta, Maria and Tobe Levin. *Kiminta. A Maasai's Fight against Female Genital Mutilation*. UnCUT/VOICES Press, 2015.

Barungi, Violet and Hilda Twongyeirwe. *Taboo. Voices of Women in Uganda on Female Genital Mutilation*. UnCUT/VOICES Press, 2015.

Table of Contents

List of Figures

Acknowledgements

This book presents the results of extensive research on Female Genital Mutilation in Iran begun in 2005 and ended in 2015. Throughout the decade-long journey, numerous people and organizations helped me to complete the project.

I wish to thank them.

The study and, in particular, parts of the fieldwork including fact-finding and field-based training were achieved only with significant support and assistance from Fatema Karimi, Behara Alvi, Nasrin Fasihi, Morad Remezani, Mehsa Tollabi, Ronak Azarbekh, Nasrin Ahmedpoor, Ali Rehmanpoor, Shirin Akbery, Shiwa Restegari, Nasrin Gehremani, Shafagh Rehmani, Zehra Daryaneverd, Fahima Minabi and Mohemmad Azizi. To you all, I say, thank you so much for helping me carry out this research on the traumatic rite of FGM.

Gratitude also belongs to those who assembled, analyzed, triangulated, and developed a narrative enabling presentation of this work in the form of a comprehensive report. My utmost thanks go to Humaira Naz. In contact with me for years despite the great distance from Pakistan and recently from Australia, she stood by this research and assisted as I developed and refined the study. Thank you, Humaira, for being such a perceptive consultant.

I wish to thank my late father as well. Together with family members and close friends, he helped me advance this project despite all the hardship and obstacles associated with it. I am also thankful to Shafagh Rehmani for sustenance in difficult times and to others who have chosen to be nameless for their cooperation and readiness to accomplish this task.

Further, I wish to acknowledge Ronak Rezaie for translating some parts of the work into English. Thanks also go to Muslim Nazemi for his help analyzing data and graphs; Said Esmaeili for designing data maps and graphs; and Shirin Talandeh, Mansour Eskandari and Dr. Shamei for their legal advice. I am also grateful to the following who briefly assisted, got involved and supported parts of this research: Pekhshan Azizi, Hirow Zobiri, Zinab Bayezidi, Parvin Zabihi, Fahimeh Hassanian, Elham Mandegari, Inna Galoyan, Mehrnoosh Pakzadeh, Shela Azizi, Jina Moderssgorji, Sehar Tebak, Rayehe Mozafarian, Muray Remezan, Fatema Deryai, Kejal Padash and Avat.

Thanks are also due to Mark Clarkson, Dr. Yaser Al Hamadi, Dr. Maria Molinero Fernández, Thomas v. der Osten-Sacken, Tini, Nadia, Jessi, Hekate Papadaki, Arvid Vormann, Falah Murad, Waris Dirie and her office, UNICEF and UNFPA Tehran and New York staff, the No FGM initiative, Dr Sarah Keeler, Kees van Der Zanden, Pauline van Norel, Louke Koopmans, Ibrahim Samin Ali, staff of the anthropology departments of the University of Kent in Canterbury UK, and the University of Tehran, the Gender department of SOAS (School of Oriental and African Studies) and archive staff at the British Library and the National Library of Iran, who have all been a great source of inspiration by providing professional guidance and assistance.

My gratitude extends to all the clerics, religious institutions and other public figures who cooperated in this research: Haji Mullaha Hassan Vazhi, Molavi Ali Reza Ilkhaniferahabadi, Mula Omer Bestaki, the office of Molavi Abdol Hamid Ismaeel Zahi, Molavi Gasam Noori, Molavi Mohammed Qeshmi, Molavi Zahed Lengaiferahani, Mula Osman Mukreyani, Qom and Mashhad Seminary of Traditional Islamic School of Higher Learning, Provincial clergy Centres of Kurdistan, West Azerbaijan and Hormozgan.

I am obliged to Dr. Helen Carr from the University of Oxford for her friendship, motivation and professional advice; Hilary Burrage, Dr. Tobe Levin and Katayune Ehsani for sharing information, proofreading and feedback, particularly in finalizing the framework of this study. Burrage and Levin also proved themselves sensitive, meticulous editors in transforming rough translation from the Farsi to polished English. Richard Lim deserves mention for his editorial support.

And last, not least, I acknowledge the care, hospitality and insights shared by all the relatives, friends and people of West Azerbaijan, Kurdistan, Kermanshah, Ilam, Sistan and Baluchestan, Golestan and Hormozgan provinces who provided team members with accommodation and help, in particular Manssor Rehmani, Saman Rehmani, Kave Kermanshai, Belal Moradvisi, Golala Behrami, Nasrin Hussini, Deyako Alvi, Nasrin Nosreti, Maryam Mulai, Leyla Anayetzadeh, Ahmed Hussini, Parvin Ferhang, Seyamek Ferhang, Hassan Fesharaki, Asmer and Ibrahim, Ahmed Bekhtaver, Jamileh Hashemyan, Kawe Rehmani Hatice Kamar, Sirin Gencer, Lale Yurtsever and Shala Najfei.

Finally, I thank you, the reader, for wanting to learn more about this dangerous tradition, hopefully in order to hasten its end.

Abstract

Our comprehensive research uncovers and analyzes Female Genital Mutilation[1] in Iran. FGM is prevalent in West Azerbaijan and in the provinces of Kurdistan, Kermanshah, and Hormozgan. A longstanding ritual, the ablation of female genitalia continues to violate aspects of women's sexual rights. It is promoted and justified by beliefs, norms, and attitudes. Political and economic systems are also implicated. While data exists on the Iranian practice, prior to this investigation, scope had been limited.

To inscribe the issue on the world's agenda, this study provides a considerable number of in-depth figures and, at the same time, offers building blocks for a comprehensive program to terminate the custom in Iran. Our recommendations will benefit practicing communities as well as the government, individuals, and NGOs who, for the first time, are provided with updated statistics. The findings also open two wider perspectives. First, the data set a baseline for future research; second, the findings reveal the very presence of FGM in Iran, a fact that many, for lack of evidence, deny. On a broader scale, they also refute the longstanding but erroneous belief that Africa is the only continent where genital wounding takes place. Finally, the information will assist civil society, children's rights lobbies and international organizations to dialogue with relevant stakeholders so that we can end, together, the exercise of *sunnet* in Iran.

---

[1] Some international agencies call it FGM/C for 'cutting'.

Prologue

Although analysts underscore the challenge of eradicating a custom that has survived for millennia, ending Female Genital Mutilation[2] is considered imperative by feminists, human rights campaigners and social activists as well as responsible governments and international organizations such as UNICEF. I join them.

Thus, the project culminating in this book started 10 years ago. Since then considerable energy has nourished the effort to learn more about the practice in Iran and to launch pilot interventions to stop it. Admittedly, where the complicated 'ritual' lurks beneath the surface, FGM is difficult to comprehend and even harder to eliminate.

My research bgan in 2005 when I returned after many years' absence from Europe to my birthplace, Iranian Kurdistan. Previously employed by humanitarian relief NGOs, I gained from my work in Africa the opportunity to observe UN projects to end genital ablation in countries like Egypt, Somalia, Kenya and Sudan. Remembering vaguely from my childhood that cutting the clitoris, locally called *sunnet*, existed in some parts of Iranian Kurdistan, I decided to research first among my own family and close relations.

The evidence shocked me. Long enduring in areas of Mukriyan[3] where I am from, *sunnet* had been suffered by my grandmothers, mother and sister. All had undergone FGM.

Now, within Iran, people from non-FGM-practicing backgrounds tend not to know the tradition exists, and as a male

---

[2] You will find some authors using a euphemism to refer to ablation of female genitalia: Female Genital Cutting or FGM/C. Throughout this study unless otherwise stated, FGM will refer to both female genital mutilation and female genital 'cutting'.

[3] Part of Iran's West Azerbaijan province, the Greater Mukriyan region encompasses several cities such as Bukan, Piranshahr, Nagadeh, Mahabad, Sardasht and Oshnaviyeh.

whose 'unusual' vita – I had lived in Africa and Europe – made me somewhat of an outsider, I encountered resistance and bewilderment when asking about this sensitive topic concerning cutting a female's private parts. The research was belittled, especially by men. Not a few with whom I spoke, including a number of relatives, felt that the project would dishonor me. No educated man would want to deal with a theme so incompatible with masculine 'pride', they felt. Here I would like once again to thank my late father. Despite the pressure of 'neighborly' viewpoints shared at times by the federal government, he supported me throughout.

As the scope of the investigation gradually grew, I began looking at regions in Iran beyond my home town. On this journey, I enjoyed a significant amount of help in fieldwork, analysis and assembly of data.

My results appear here in book form for the first time. While focused on areas most affected by FGM in the western part of the country, namely West Azerbaijan, Kurdistan and Kermanshah provinces, and some areas of southern Iran, namely Hormozgan and its islands, I provide a comprehensive overview of prevalence in the entire country.

While always anticipating book production, I also filmed research activities such as interviews and talks, producing the first and so far only documentary about FGM in Iran, *In the Name of Tradition*. The footage captures viewpoints of residents in various Kurdish neighborhoods in the city of Mahabad, in nearby Kurdistan and in Hawraman, located where Kurdistan and Kermanshah provinces meet. A revised version of the movie adds anthropological material from Kermanshah and Hormozgan province, including the islands Qeshm, Hormuz and Kish. Featuring local women and *bibis*, i.e. women cutters, the camera also shows local men, medical staff and clerics talking about FGM, providing an eloquent illustrative record of the custom in less-visited and infrequently reported rural areas of Iran.

In my view, *sunnet* and the hidden beliefs behind it violate human rights in general and women and children's rights in particular. Hence it is incumbent upon everyone to eradicate it. The great news is that FGM rates are declining, albeit too slowly, across the globe, including in the secret pockets in Iran. Thus, work remains to be done.

Where do the difficulties lie? My years of research and participation in interventions lead me to conclude that ending FGM requires full cooperation of all parties. That is why I encourage the state to take a stand and work hand in hand with activists, international institutions and local forces. To gain support for a joint plan to address FGM in Iran, colleagues and I have been reaching out for years to responsible ministries and provincial officials. Our labors, however, have not yet born fruit.

Nonetheless, like-minded associates and I will continue proposing a nationwide awareness-raising effort to promote community involvement, dialogue with stakeholders, and synchronize action with our universal human rights commitments. I will be happy to provide the needed data about affected provinces to Iranian ministries and agencies, including those responsible for overseeing the health sector, social services and medical universities.

After all, Tehran has signed a number of international children's rights treaties, and while the nation should ratify any outstanding conventions, it also needs to adopt a comprehensive action plan against FGM. Such a blueprint should include engagement of local influencers and spokespersons (given the culturally sensitive nature of the topic); a national education program focusing on health risks and other dangers associated with FGM; and new laws criminalizing genital cuts. (For further recommendations see chapter four.) To succeed, the government can look to UNICEF and benefit from capabilities of NGOs and Community Based Organizations (CBOs) in Iran.

As noted, I'm convinced that only teamwork involving politicians, activists, international institutions and local communities can give hope of fully wiping out this scourge.

* * * * *

This book consists of four chapters. Following the acknowledgment and prologue, chapter one defines FGM, explains terms and lists types. It then examines the historical roots of the 'rite' and examines constitutive, influential factors. To conclude, it offers an overview of FGM prevalence, noting limited evidence of a minimally declining trend worldwide.

The second chapter focuses on FGM in Iran, describes relevant studies, introduces my research and presents findings. It portrays the regions and villages in which cutting prevails and relays inhabitants' beliefs (and rationalizations) about the practice. Finally, I outline efforts made so far to fight the tradition and include my own pilot interventions.

The third chapter chronicles worldwide campaigns and legal action against FGM, including current jurisprudence affecting genital ablation of girls in Iran. It also examines the potential for change, including relevant Islamic law.

The fourth chapter, offering conclusions, lessons learned and additional experience, addresses its recommendations to affected communities and responsible government representatives such as those in health, education and social services.

The massive amount of data gathered during a decade of research has yet to be fully analyzed, but the intention to publish it as a book in English plus, eventually, in Farsi and Kurdish is coming to fruition. Similarly, I plan to release a study of child marriage in Iran, begun some years ago and based on data that emerged while investigating FGM.

Let me now invite my readers, and in particular Iranian readers, to refrain from passing hasty judgment and to meet this provocative report with open minds.

Photo 1. Holy City of Qom, capital of Qom province.
(Credit: Kameel Ahmady)

CHAPTER ONE

History and Prevalence
of FGM in the World

"I do not wish them to have power over men; but over themselves."

Mary Wollstonecraft.

A Vindication of the Rights of Woman. (*1792*)

An ancient ritual, female genital mutilation violates essential aspects of women's and children's sexual (and human) rights. Recent United Nations Children's Fund (UNICEF) data indicate that roughly 200 million girls and women alive today have undergone some form of FGM. 92 million are over the age of 10 and most live in Africa. According to official UN figures, the practice exists in 29 countries in western, eastern, and north-eastern Africa, in parts of the Middle East and Asia, and within immigrant communities in Europe, North America and Australia (EndFGM, 2012; UNICEF, 2013). Prevalence in several nations of origin exceeds 80% (UNICEF, 2014). The age for undergoing genital wounding varies from one culture to another. In general, a girl is at greatest risk between 4 and 12; however, some groups amputate the clitoris of newborns or mature women just prior to marriage or in parturition.

Female Genital Mutilation: terms and definitions

The tradition generally involves partial or, less often, total removal of external female genitalia. In English, the term "female circumcision" has been applied to these ablations, but the implied parallel to male circumcision is problematic. Nowadays, the work of feminist activists has led to a broad consensus: female genital mutilation (FGM) is the preferred expression.[4] The most common and acceptable typology is that of the World Health Organization (WHO), which divides the abuse into four types.

Type I, the mildest, comes in two forms. The first removes the prepuce (clitoral hood) or partially or totally amputates the visible shaft of the clitoris including, of course, the foreskin. The second form is called clitoridectomy (WHO, 2008).

Type II is the partial or total ablation of the labia minora, with or without amputation of the clitoral glans and labia majora. It is subdivided into three forms: excision of the labia minora; deletion of the clitoral glans and the labia minora; elimination of the clitoral glans, the labia minora and the labia majora (WHO, 2008).

Type III inflicts the most painful and extensive wound that ablates the external genitalia and fuses – by infibulating or sewing up -- the labia, leaving only a small opening at the perineum's posterior for voiding urine and menstrual blood. Type III has two forms. The first removes and closes the labia minora; the second does the same with the labia majora (WHO, 2008) using thorns, catgut, surgical thread or poultices. Afterward, the victim's legs are laced together for two to six weeks. "Although only an estimated 15-20% of all women who experience genital mutilation undergo type III, in certain countries such as Djibouti, Somalia and Sudan the proportion is 80 to [well above] 90%. Labor entails further cutting to open a passage for the infant and is usually followed by sealing afterwards." Infibulation is imposed on a smaller scale in parts of

---

[4] Some critique the term "circumcision" for females since it links FGM with circumcision proper or cutting around the foreskin of the penis, a different procedure with contrasting aims. Thus, critics say, the word circumcision applied to females conceals the violence of FGM by nesting it within a familiar category; they contend that opposition should dispense with the term "circumcision" altogether in the female context. I don't fully agree because the male/female conceptual distinction may be important to people who value the process. I would however emphasize that girls are cut, highlighting the underage status of victims. My main objection is to an extremely painful, unjustified tradition, generally performed in unhygienic conditions and without aftercare. Thus, imposed on children, it violates their rights.

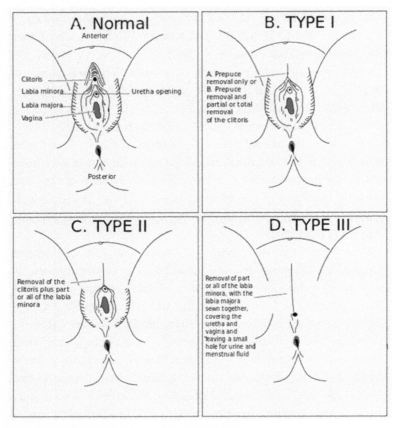

Figure 1. Normal Vagina and Types of FGM.
(Credit: WHO, 2008).

Egypt, Eritrea, Ethiopia, Gambia, Kenya and Mali, and may occur in other communities where information is lacking or is still incomplete (WHO, 2008).[5]

Type IV covers all other procedures that harm healthy female genitalia such as pricking, piercing, incising, scraping and cauterizing.

---

[5] *Eliminating Female Genital Mutilation: An Inter-Agency Statement.*
http://apps.who.int/iris/bitstream/10665/43839/1/9789241596442_eng.pdf
Accessed 22 August 2016.

A second common classification differs slightly from the above. It divides FGM into three types: *sunnah* circumcision, female genital mutilation and Pharaonic circumcision corresponding loosely to the previous typology (Alsibiani and Rouzi, 2010).

Conditions and Effects of FGM

FGM is practiced mainly without either anesthesia or the girl's consent, and her struggles can amplify the severity of pain. Unhygienic conditions often prevail, and victims tend to be young children. It is typically performed by a traditional circumciser, mostly a woman, with no medical background or training, whose only qualification is her (not inconsiderable) years of experience. She may use razor blades, scissors or knives and then, if type 3, thread or similar adhesive to close the wound. Significantly, although medicalization has become a serious issue in some nations, FGM in Iran tends to be carried out not in hospitals or clinics but rather in non-sterile village environments.

Not surprisingly, FGM impairs a girl's physical and psychological health; it can even take the victim's life or cause disabilities that last for years. Although practicing communities claim health benefits of the procedure, WHO, UNICEF, UNESCO, the UN General Assembly and other UN organs have announced in a joint statement that FGM has no known medical advantage. On the contrary. Its perverse effects are multiple and dangerous, interfering with basic bodily functions.

Type I, said to 'merely' prick but not remove the clitoris, is less prone to cause damage later on, but more excessive 'surgeries' blight health due to severe pain which neuro-scientists have shown destroys brain cells; complications in childbirth; difficulties in urination and in sexual intercourse; reduction of sexual pleasure and multiple physical and psychological issues. Cutting the female genital also increases the probability of infection, can cause Hepatitis B, and transmit HIV or other viruses. Women whose vulva has suffered such abuse show a higher prevalence of pelvic inflammation and this in turn can affect fertility. Statistically, the number of barren women among those who have suffered FGM type III exceeds others.

Although no intervention guarantees complete recovery, plastic surgery now treats injuries and returns a degree of sexual sensitivity. While only a few centimeters of clitoris protrude from the body and are therefore exposed to the blade, the clitoral root remains, and, although perception of pleasurable stimulation along its length diminishes, the long organ is amenable to restoration.

Historical Roots of FGM

Despite considerable research by historians and anthropologists, the history of FGM remains unknown. Several sources that have traced it back more than 2000 years generally point to ancient Egypt, specifically around the Nile, as the geographic heartland of its spread.

More precisely, it is considered to be a Pharaonic practice dating from the 5th century BC. "Pharaonic circumcision," an expression prevalent in popular discourse, is sometimes considered proof of the claim. Several researchers suggest that early Egyptians infibulated women to prevent pregnancy, especially among slaves. Others mention the practice as an African Stone Age method of "protecting" young females from rape (Lightfoot-Klein, 1983; Iweulmor and Veney, 2006). Early Roman and Arabic civilizations linked FGM to virginity and chastity; in ancient Rome female captives were subjected to it to repress sexual activity and to raise their market value (Iweulmor and Veney, 2006).

Despite its obscure origins, FGM spread throughout the world where it can be found to this day. Not limited to Africa and the Middle East, ablation of female genitalia was performed by Australian Aboriginal communities, the Phoenicians, the Hittites, the Ethiopians, and ethnic groups in Amazonia, some parts of India, Pakistan, Malaysia, and Indonesia as well as in the Philippines. As late as the nineteenth and into the twentieth century, FGM was also known in Europe and the US where some physicians prescribed clitoridectomy to prevent masturbation or thwart lesbianism and treat mental disorders such as hysteria (Brown, 1866). In fact, FGM sporadically continued in the USA until the 1970s in one form or another. Pulitzer prize-winning novelist Alice Walker, for instance, included FGM performed on US soil in her pioneering novel against female mutilation, *Possessing the Secret of Joy* [1992].)

FGM: global prevalence

UNICEF confirms that FGM is most common in twenty-nine countries in Africa as well as in Asia and the Middle East. No evidence exists for it as indigenous to southern Africa or in Arabic-speaking North Africa, except Egypt. Increased migration from practicing regions, however, has brought excision to other parts of the world including Australia, Canada, New Zealand, the US and Europe (Boyle and Preves, 2000). To a lesser extent, clitoridectomy continues in Indonesia, Malaysia, Pakistan, India, Iraq and Iran – as this research will show.

In Iraq, Sunni Kurds, some Arabs and Turkmens subject girls to the blade. A 2005 survey by WADI, a German NGO, estimates 60% FGM prevalence among Kurds in Iraq (Ghareeb and Dougherty, 2004, 226) but later studies from the same area, following the launch of local and regional campaigns, show a lower figure, suggesting success. According to the Kurdish regional government, UNICEF and local NGOs, FGM rates have indeed been going down (UNICEF, 2014).

Reliable data on the prevalence of FGM is increasingly available. UNICEF's statistical review reveals the numbers collected in Demographic and Health Surveys (DHS) for six countries: the Central African Republic, Côte d'Ivoire, Egypt, Eritrea, Mali and Sudan. In these nations, the rate among reproductive-age women varies from 43% to 97% with data also subdivided according to ethnic groups. As for the United States, responding to the urging of Jaha Dukureh, President Obama has promised to launch the nation's first-ever demographic survey. Statistics are presently silent about FGM in Europe as well, though 500,000 women and girls residing there are estimated to have suffered it or to be at risk today.

The map confirms the 'rite' in the abovementioned countries and shows that Iraq, at 8%, has amongst the lowest rates of FGM (UNICEF, 2013). Nonetheless, that nation has now found its place on the list.

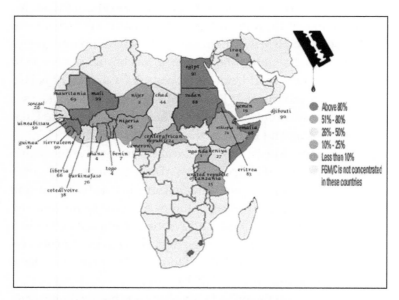

Figure 2. Prevalence of FGM in selected African nations. (Credit: UNICEF, 2013).

The Politics of FGM: Motivations, Justifications, Rationalisations

Embedded in the social fabric of practicing communities, the custom elicits a plethora of reasons to justify removing a part of women's bodies that men do not possess. These pronouncements derive from the ideologies and histories of the groups involved, founded on gender inequalities. Many theorists believe the main motive is to control women's sexuality under patriarchy. In other words, institutionalized male supremacy is the bedrock. Without it, FGM would be cut off at the root, a hypothesis that underscores the usefulness of feminist analysis.

At the same time, motives are complicated by cultural and religious convictions that drive individuals to ablate female genitalia, including indigenous judgments on erotic behavior, beauty, health, and chastity. The following passages survey justifications that perpetuate FGM.

Many, for instance, hold a (totally erroneous) belief that FGM stimulates fertility in women, decreases sexual – including homosexual – urges, and increases loyalty to the bride's arranged groom. Thus, it is thought, infibulation preserves the woman's virginity and ensures fidelity toward her husband, a warrant achieved by stitching her vagina to be unsealed exclusively by the spouse on the wedding night. Beyond guaranteeing the organ's delivery in a pristine state, infibulation, by tightening the orifice, affords extra sexual pleasure to the man, thus serving male desire. Interestingly, those communities that integrate FGM into their initiation ceremonies reinforce the link between mutilation and the sexual intercourse that quickly follows on attaining (socially enforced) 'maturity' and subsequent wedded 'bliss'.

FGM supporters who claim it empowers their daughters understand it as ensuring marriage – an economic arrangement – and the girls' ability to protect the family's good name. Practicing communities' cultural beliefs about gender and sexuality also bolster FGM. Many associate the procedure with loveliness, modesty and cleanliness in women, strongly implying that, unshorn, a female will be ugly, salacious and sullied. Never far from the surface appears the underlying motive, as mentioned, to limit and control women's sexual comportment. Where virginity is required to enter the conjugal state, freedom from erotic experience is valued (in men, too, but more in women). Thus, the cut is thought to minimize passion outside wedlock but, by corollary, oddly ceases to do so once vows have been exchanged. And it is true, a girl who has undergone FGM receives more proposals than the outlier left intact.

Indeed, as noted, supporting beliefs associate genital erasure with hygiene, aesthetics, and definitions of gender. In FGM-practicing communities, for instance, an unmutilated woman is considered impure and her genitalia unsightly. The fear that her clitoris will grow also enters into play, for how can a woman have an appendage to rival a man's? Some societies contend, moreover, that food cooked by women who are not 'circumcised' is not halal, opening the door to contentious arguments over Islam's role in FGM.

Although genital ablation predates Islam, Christianity and Judaism, you often find FGM linked to religion as an Islamic requirement.[6] This attitude, however, is in error, at least as far as the leading schools of theology are concerned. Granted, FGM is prevalent in certain Christian and Muslim communities and, formerly, also among the Jewish Beta Israel (known in Ethiopia as Falasha, meaning 'stranger'). But FGM is not mentioned in either the *Quran* or the Bible, nor is it described in any authoritative Jewish, Christian or Islamic texts. Thus the custom is not constituted by religions even if some communities mistakenly think it is, perhaps due to ideas about female 'purity' that patriarchal faiths uphold. Being devout in the

---

[6] Besides certain groups of Christians, Muslims and, earlier, Jews, FGM is also widespread among animists and other local religions.

Creator's eyes can seem to justify the anti-sexual ablations of the 'impure' organ.

But perhaps among all motives, more cogent than religion is economics. In some (though by no means all) groups, an uncut girl is seen as a family burden because non-compliance with the deeply rooted mutilating practice makes her ineligible to wed. This results in her inability to fetch the 'bride price' for her parents. In addition, understanding their behavior as a religious duty, clerics (both men and women), community leaders, village chiefs, traditional birth attendants, and 'circumcisers' promote FGM in rural areas; the cutters, of course, wish to ensure a regular income.[7]

FGM: A Declining Trend

Current waves of modernization, media outreach and growing awareness have changed attitude towards FGM and altered behavior. Nonetheless, peoples in Diaspora may contravene domestic progress when, for instance, they maintain FGM as a marker of difference from the host population and continue to see it not as injury but as a service to the child. A famous Dutch film calls it "an act of love."

International development and humanitarian organizations look at the issue, however, as violence against women and children, in NGO-speak as VAW (Violence against Women). The UN describes FGM as a "manifestation of deep-rooted gender inequality that assigns [women] an inferior position in society." As a result, over the past decade, significant efforts to promote gender equality have been made at global and regional level. Even a number of *exciseuses – dayas* or, in Iran, *bibis –* have come out against the practice.

---

[7] As chapter four will show, cutters' cooperation is critical for prevention, and the attitudes of these actors can be influenced by, for example, retraining for opportunities to supplement lost income. Hence at grassroots level, development workers collaborate closely with birth attendants to convince them to oppose the practice.

Thus, ideological advances against VAW have begun, in many countries, to weaken the demand for cutting. One contributing factor is the increasing openness with which the topic is presently discussed. You find it in print and electronic media as well as on the streets. In 2014, the UK hosted the first Girl Summit (Girl Summit, 2014) aimed at mobilizing domestic and international efforts to end, in a generation, FGM as well as child, early and forced marriage (CEFM). UNICEF co-hosted the Girl Summit, welcoming participants from around the world, gathering UN agencies, survivors, charities, community

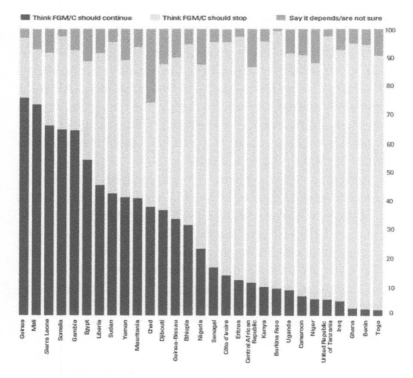

Figure 3. Modest reduction in new cases of FGM in 2,000 communities across Africa. (Credit: UNICEF, 2013)

groups, faith leaders and front-line professionals, raising a significant amount of funding – £25 million – and convincing many who had supported FGM to join the movement against it, evidence that the trend toward eradication has begun. Breaking the omerta – the unspoken taboo on talking about FGM in media, in private and in public – plays a major role (see Figure 3, page 26).

With growing conviction, campaigns now widely disseminate information and encourage debate. In some of the world's most affected areas, we see positive changes in orientation leading to a drop, if minimal, in the rate of cutting. For instance, a recent study by the Demographic Health Surveys in Yemen indicates a decline in the practice due to efforts by government and other relevant stakeholders (Al-Khulaidi et al., 2013).

Similarly, for decades in Burkina Faso, First Lady Chantal Campaoré has been outspoken against excision, and the state's leaders have explicitly acknowledged FGM as a women's and children's rights issue, adopting unique strategies to tackle it. They combine education, protection, and prosecution (UNICEF, 2013; 114) and were among the first to set up a hotline that facilitates speedy police mediation to stop imminent abuse. Moreover, governments in Iraq and Egypt have made a few arrests and, in some cases, fined practitioners. In Iraq, a UNICEF survey of hundreds of families in the Kurdish region also shows a decrease of 31% in FGM. And best of all, among adolescent girls, the procedure has almost halved in Benin, the Central African Republic, Liberia and Nigeria (UNICEF, 2013).

Another UN report in 2012 shows, with the exception of Mauritania, overall, a modest if nonetheless encouraging reduction in new cases of FGM in 2,000 communities across Africa, evidence of change (Pandit, 2012) as shown in the following graph.

Rates dropping: FGM/C prevalence percentage change

Joint Programme countries where comparison is available, women aged 15-49

	-20 -15 -10 -5 0 5	
2003 to 2009	-15.8%	Kenya
2005 to 2010	-8.9%	Senegal
2000 to 2005	-7.0%	Ethiopia
2001 to 2006	-7.0%	Mali
2000 to 2008	-6.4%	Egypt
1995 to 2002	-6.1%	Eritrea
2003 to 2006	-5.4%	Burkina Faso
1999 to 2005	-3.0%	Guinea
2000 to 2006	-1.1%	Sudan
2000 to 2007	+1.3%	Mauritania

Figure 4. Rates dropping: FGM prevalence percentage change. (Credit: UNICEF, 2013)

CHAPTER TWO

Prevalence of FGM in Iran

Although neither exclusively Muslim nor Middle Eastern, 'female circumcision' undeniably occurs in certain communities and nations associated with Sunnis of the Shafi'i school of Islamic jurisprudence. In Iran, type 1 according to WHO typology has a long history, and many people continue to understand FGM as a ritual maintained for reasons of faith and culture.[8] Although mainly in rural areas, it also occurs in urban outskirts and parts of both the east and west of the country. More precisely, in Iran (and Iraq), Shafi'i Kurds who speak the Sorani dialect rather than Kurmanji[9] are most likely to ablate girls' genitalia.

In Iran today, the Twelver Shia branch of Islam is the official state religion; 90-95% of the population identifies as Shia. The minority Sunni Iranian community totals about 4% to 8%, mainly Kurds and Baluchs as well as Persian groupings in the south and Turkmen of northern Iran (Cheng and Beigi, 2012). The remaining 2% comprise non-Muslim religious minorities (Ameli and Molaei, 2012).

Although FGM in Iranian Kurdistan is imposed in certain areas including villages near the border with Iraqi Kurdistan,

---

[8] The four provinces where FGM is known to exist also have a history of violence against women such as child and forced marriage, polygamy and 'honor' killings. Cultural and traditional influences sometimes lead as well to the self-immolation of women (Keddie, 2000).

[9] The Kurdish language has various dialects, but two groups stand out: Kermanji Kurdish and Surani Kurdish. Kermanji is the dominant tongue of Syria, Turkey and a part of Northern Iraqi Kurdistan. It is also spoken by Kurds in the North and West of Iran. You will hear Surani in regions near Iraq's Suleimanieh, Iraqi Kurdistan, south of Western Azerbaijan and also Kermanshah, Ilam and Iraq's Khaanghin. Other Kurdish dialects include Kermanshahi, Ilaami, Laki and Kalhori.

prevalence is patchy and varies sharply from one region to another. For instance, in some cases, you find the custom in one village but not in its closest neighbor whose inhabitants are unaware that the girls next door are being cut.

This secrecy feeds denial characteristic of the issue in Iran. Government representatives, officials, Pan-Iranist individuals and groups refuse to acknowledge its presence on their soil. Not surprisingly, then, neither the regime nor civil society associations have made any serious effort to stop it. Government is especially remiss, not having commissioned any comprehensive research nor passed legislation even though a law against FGM would provide opportunities and support activists. Not surprisingly, then, no public awareness-raising program exists either. So far we have seen an opposite approach, to sweep the issue under the rug.

The next chapter looks at exemplary efforts recently made elsewhere by international institutions, states, activists and NGOs to end the toxic habit. Even in the Middle East, the Kurdish Regional Government (KRG) in Iraq, assisted by local charities and global organizations, has for years seen relative success in reducing the incidence of ablations (HRW, 2010). This advocacy stands in stark contrast to Iran where, as we have just noted, FGM is still not publicly discussed and is seldom even privately mentioned. Iranian media are not permitted to touch the subject. Apparently the Shi'a religious establishment lacks interest in tackling the problem, unwilling to involve itself in an exclusively Sunni practice (EndFGM, 2012).

These observations notwithstanding, compared to its predecessors, the Rouhani administration has paid increased attention to social problems and issues of family, children and welfare. It has listened to the outcry of social activists and researchers by fulfilling a presidential election promise to consult the public. A 20-page draft of its proposed Charter of Citizen's Rights, which is being billed as a huge advance for civil rights in Iran, is evidence of this commitment.

Despite progress, however, FGM continues unexamined in universities in Iran. A handful of postgraduate theses notwithstanding, we find virtually no independent research or publications in Farsi. Lacking government support and for reasons of security, only a limited number of serious, comprehensive studies have been conducted. Parallel to this neglect in the educational sector is the total lack of public funding for awareness-raising in affected regions; in fact, the few proposals put forward privately have been denied permission to proceed. This explains why we have no epidemiological study nor pilot project to determine the exact prevalence of FGM or measure the impact of pedagogy and training to fight it.

Most of the studies below were conducted by non-local female university students investigating small samples ranging from 40 to 200 or 400 cases, and most of these probes resemble each other in size, method, and approach. They give greater emphasis to general information and less to analyses and solutions.

Several Relevant Research Studies

Homa Ahadi, majoring in midwifery, conducted research in some of Minab's medical centers in Hormozgan province. Her 2002 report, *Prevalence, awareness and attitudes: FGM in Minab*, may be the first such study of the issue in Iran. Having examined and interviewed 400 adult females aged 15 to 49 from the Minab region, Ms. Ahadi found Type 1 and some Type 2 FGM cases. She concludes that incidence can be reduced by increasing awareness of the intervention's dangers, ensuring medical care, promoting education, and changing perceptions

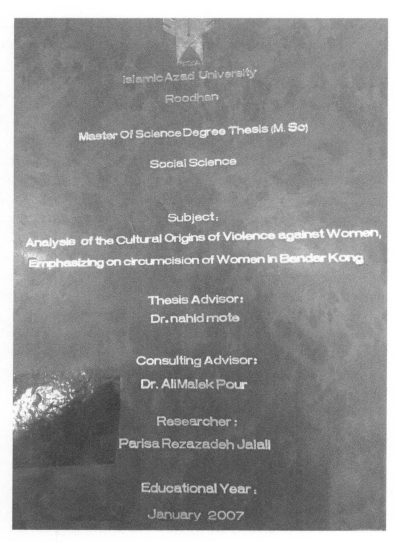

Photo 2. Paiza Rezazadeh Jalali's thesis.
(Credit: Kameel Ahmady)

of gender. Some parts of this study were subsequently published in *The Journal of Qazin University of Medical Sciences* and later in the *International Journal of Gynecology & Obstetrics* (Ahadi et al., 2009).

Further studies followed.

In 2007 a social science postgraduate at Islamic Azad University of Roodhan, Paisa Rezazadeh Jalali wrote *Analysis of the Cultural Origins of Violence against Women, with an Emphasis on the Circumcision of Women in Bandar Kong*. Randomly choosing 200 case studies at a medical center in Bandar Kong, Hormozgan province, she focused primarily on two factors: religion and education. The data confirm that stronger support for FGM exists among the Sunni than among the Shi'a, even though a minority of Shi'a women practiced and believed in FGM as well. Her results further suggest an important role for education among women; advanced schooling correlated with increased likelihood of refusal to 'circumcise' daughters and opposition to cutting (Jalali, 2007). Moreover, when Jalali analyzed cultural and religious reasons for 'female circumcision' in Bandar Kong, she concluded that the practice exemplifies sexual violence against women performed under cover of religious beliefs and traditions. Some of her informants, for instance, believe FGM is allowed under Islam and also deserves divine rewards. In Jalali's view, the Iranian government appears unaware of its obligations concerning human rights, another reason for such violence. She ends, however, on a hopeful note, that most women in the area she studied now feel that girls' 'circumcision' lacks any benefit but is instead harmful to its victims.

Another study that focuses on FGM among Iran's Kurds is one of few examinations of the subject at university level. Fatimah Karimi wrote her postgraduate thesis while working toward a master's degree in women's studies at Allameh Taba-

taba'i University in Tehran in 2009. Although during the final preparatory stage university officials rejected the thesis, claiming the topic was inappropriate and far too sensitive, the following year permission was granted to print. The work then appeared under the colophon of women's studies publisher Roshangaran. Excepting a limited number of medical articles in credible journals (Karimi, 2010), this was the first time the Minister of Culture and Islamic Guidance had ever acquiesced to bringing out a book on FGM. The Iranian government had not been keen to allow publications on the topic.

Photo 3. Fatimah Karimi.
Tragedy of the Body.
Tehran: Roshengeran, 2010.
(Credit: Kameel Ahmady)

Compared to Jalali, Fatimah Karimi provides more in-depth research, analyzing face to face interviews with 40 adult women in and around the Pava Town region in Kermanshah province. Her method consisted of targeting likely subjects and then 'snow balling', i.e. asking for further introductions. The study provides a global history of FGM and international actions to prevent it, presenting various arguments by feminists and sociologists and quotes from other work on the topic including data on excision for the region of West Azerbaijan and Kurdistan provinces that I had collected (Ahmady, 2006). My data demonstrate the custom's negative sequelae on the body and mind of girls and reveal a declining trend in Kurdish areas.

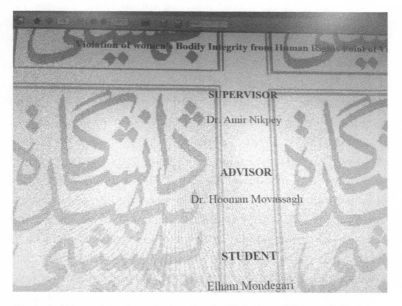

Photo 4. Elham Mandegari's MA thesis. Violation of Women's Bodily Integrity from a Human Rights Perspective. *Tehran: Shehid Beheshti University, 2013. (Credit: Kameel Ahmady)*

*Photo 5. Health Promotion Perspectives.
(Credit: Kameel Ahmady)*

Karimi concludes by calling for further studies and increased data collection. Sharing research results with schools and treatment centers would increase awareness on the part of the general public, she points out. Religious figures should also be encouraged to play a role, making the mosque a place for preaching against FGM and for vitiating weak religious justifications.

A law student from Shahid Beheshti University in Tehran, Elham Mandegari is the first to base her work on clear legal points and, most important, family law, Islamic law and the penal code. Her master's thesis *Violation of Women's Bodily Integrity from a Human Rights Perspective* drew on limited fieldwork in the west and south of Iran, in which she solicited the views of local women, men, and clerics. She also included a large number of references to the opinions of eminent scholars and religious actors as well as quotations from imams and from the *Quran* itself. Some of these passages suggest that, if ever there was a reason for the practice, it no longer exists (Mandegari, 2008). The somatic and mental impairment excised girls suffer backs her up as she argues that no deviation from human rights for the sake of cultural diversity is justified. FGM clearly violates the right to bodily integrity and physical

Photo 6. Rayehe Mozafarian. A Survey on socio-cultural factors related to Female genital Mutilation: A case study of women 15-49 on Qeshm Island. *Published as an e-book,* Blade and Tradition. *Naa Kojaa website. (Credit: Kameel Ahmady)*

ISLAMIC AZAD UNIVERSITY
Central Tehran Branch
Faculty of Law - Department of
International Law Group
Law M · A Thesis
International Law

SUBJECT:
Forbidden of female Genital mutilation
(FGM) in International documents with
emphasizes on involved countries

ADVISOR:
Dr. Behshid Arfania

READER:
Dr. Atefeh Amininia

By: Fahimeh Hassanian

Summer 2012

Photo 7. Fahimeh Hassanian's thesis.
(Credit: Kameel Ahmady)

health as well as the right to 'freedom from torture or other cruel, inhumane and degrading punishment', to borrow wording from UN documents. Now, all types of mutilation, including medicalization (which some consider a means of reducing trauma), undermine the physical, spiritual, and personal well-being and security of women and children. International law regarding universal human rights cannot therefore accommodate cultural relativism in this respect, for the principle of cultural diversity applies only where it does not conflict with human rights, whereas mutilating female genitalia does indeed violate these (Mandegari, 2008).

Thus, in Mandegari's view, the regime is mandated to protect the human rights of citizens and to support groups in danger. This duty extends to strengthening the role of the UN and other international organizations in their efforts to guarantee

Photo 8. Screen shot. Chiman Rahmani sings against FGM, child-and forced marriage, violence against women.
https://www.youtube.com/watch?v=z_-QD4X6cSI [Accessed 5 August 2016] (Credit: Kameel Ahmady)

good governance. Mandegari shows the significance at this level of institutions in eradicating FGM and by implication suggests that a lack of political management is the most telling reason for its continuation in Iran.

Amplifying these scholars' work is another contribution to the topic. At the 4th National and 1st International Congress on Health, Education and Promotion, organized by the Faculty of Health and Nutrition and Nutrition Research Center of Tabriz University of Medical Sciences in 2011, T. Pashaei, F. Majlessi and A. Rahimi presented "Prevalence of Female Genital Mutilation and the Effects of Health Education based on a Behavioural Intention Model, on Attitudes and Behaviours in Women referring to Health Centres in Ravansar-Iran." The paper appeared in the conference proceedings. The initial cross-sectional part of the study involved 348 women referred to five health centers in Kermanshah province. Data analysis included both descriptive statistics and the Pearson correlation coefficient. The second, experimental part of the study featured an educational intervention on 50 women who had suffered FGM. Referencing foreign sources that show positive outcomes from communal decisions to ban FGM (Pashaei et al., 2011), the researchers concluded that ending the practice requires participation of religious leaders and custodians of health.

The year 2011 also witnessed a second study. Rayehe Mozafarian, demographics major in the Department of Economics at Shiraz University, submitted her master's thesis on FGM: *A survey on social-cultural factors related to Female Genital Mutilation: A case study of women aged 15-49 on Qeshm Island*. The researcher, active in districts and villages, distributed 400 questionnaires in medical centers. Local patrons, assisted by staff, completed them. Using quantitative research methods and techniques to compile data and determine findings, Mozafarian explored demographics, social and other indicator-based questions (Mozafarian, 2011). She identified

> ... significant relations between Female Genital Mutilation and the following independent variables: job, education, experience of Female Genital Mutilation in the family, women's use of media, sexual control of women, women's attitudes, age and marital status. In contrast, results [revealed] no significant relations between the following dependent and independent variables: other forms of violence in the family, number and gender of children. (Mozafarian, 2011)

In 2013, the thesis was published as an e-book by "Naa Kojaa," a publishing website.[10]

The final thesis on FGM in Iran to appear prior to publication of this book, authored by Fahimeh Hassanian, a postgraduate in the department of international law, Islamic Azad University of Tehran, is titled "Prohibition of Female Genital Mutilation (FGM) in International Documents with Emphasis on [affected] Countries." Although resembling Elham Mandegari's treatise on FGM with respect to international jurisprudence, Hassanian offers less information and analysis yet provides valuable insights. Incorporating facts that my research had uncovered (Ahmady, 2006), she examines global legislation against FGM, reviews parliamentary efforts and suggests strategic options. Critical of government inaction, she writes: "Various forms of FGM are found in some areas of our country (Adeniran) but sadly, so far, Tehran has neglected an issue universally considered ... a matter of human rights. The government should undertake all necessary measures to protect women from cruelty. Needed are not only regulations but also

---

[10] For further information on Rayehe Mozafarian, see pp.77-79 in Hilary Burrage. (2016) *Female Mutilation. The truth behind the horrifying global practice of female genital mutilation.* Sydney: New Holland.

penalties for those who engage in this criminal behavior." Moreover, she calls for "financial and non-financial compensation for victims," asking rhetorically, "Is FGM a crime in international instruments, or is it perceived merely as an excuse for recommendations and suggestions? If law recognizes FGM as an international crime, where is the prosecution? ... Evidence of the obligation to prohibit FGM on the part of States is lacking. [I argue that], because today, in many nations, legal and social support for protection of women and girls who are the intended victims of female genital mutilation exists, decisions based on fundamental principles must be taken by regimes responsible for breaching international commitments" (Hassanian, 2012).

In addition to the prominent work of the above mentioned scholars, you can find a number of news-style articles and pieces written on this issue in Iran. Generally, once a year, on International Zero Tolerance to FGM Day, February 6th, media features the topic even if, inside Iran, coverage remains scanty because many journalists fear reprisals for breaking the (unwritten) rules. Nonetheless, courageous articles appear and interviews are granted to Farsi-speaking media outlets or feminist websites located outside Iran.

Parvin Zabihi, who campaigns for women's rights in Kurdistan province, has also undertaken fieldwork in and around the town of Marivan where she found FGM in a certain number of Hawaram villages. She concurs that cutting stems from men's desire to subjugate women and is another sign of injustice rooted in unbalanced power relationships between the sexes, resulting in men's sovereignty over women's bodies. You can hear her in a number of radio and online interviews talking about FGM.

Innovative media is brought to bear on campaigns in still another form. For the first time in Iran, a music video against FGM by singer and artist Miss Chiman Rahmani, subtitled in English, aired on most Kurdish TV stations. Rahmani's six-minute clip, now posted on YouTube, covers FGM and child/ forced marriage. Similarly, Professor Mehrangiz Kar, a human rights lawyer and writer, covered FGM in some of her work and through media interviews. She concurs: FGM is one of many forms of women's rights violations.

Now, following this brief overview of the most important extant research on the issue, we'll turn to the present study and its findings.

Our study: FGM in Iran

As noted, comprehensive research undertaken in Iran shows that genital cutting takes place in rural parts of three western and one southern province: West Azerbaijan (Kurdish population in the south), Kurdistan, Kermanshah and Hormozgan with its islands. Iranian Kurdistan is populated by a Sunni Shafi'i majority and a few Shi'a communities. The remaining provinces have mixed Sunni, Shi'a and other ethnic and religious groups. In these regions you also find substantial minorities of Shi'a Turkish Aziri and small minorities of Turkish Ahl-e-Haq (in West Azerbaijan, between the towns of Mahabad and Miandoab), plus a minor community of Armenian Christians in Urumiye and Shi'a Kurdish Kalhor as well as Ahl-e-Haq Kurds in parts of Kermanshah who do not practice FGM. However, some Shi'a women residing near Sunni-populated areas in Hormozgan province are currently subjected to FGM; and, historically, some Shi'a Kurdish women in parts of Kermanshah and Ilam province have been excised.

This variety notwithstanding, it is important to stress that the custom is mainly associated with Sunni Kurds of the Shafi'i sect who speak the Sorani dialect, and not those in the Kurdish Kermanji-speaking areas of Iran, Iraq, Turkey and Syrian Kurdistan, even though they are also Shafi'i Muslims. In contrast, the Ahl-e-Haq Kurds, Alevi, Yezidis or Kurdish minority of Armenia as well as the forcibly migrated Kurds of the east and north of Iran *do* perform FGM.[11] Thus, the practice in Iranian Kurdistan is geographically scattered.

As we have seen, most common in Iran is the kind of wounding the World Health Organization classifies as type 1 which entails either amputating the tip of the clitoris, 'merely' pricking it, or circumcising the prepuce without ablation of the organ. The latter appears most common, at least in theory, and is understood as simply following tradition. In other words, Iranian forms of the practice remove a part of the clitoral hood. Nevertheless, how this practice is executed depends on the circumciser. Her hand may tremble, for instance, and can produce a deeper cut. The child's struggles can also cause more extensive wounding than intended.

It is therefore important to highlight that genital cutting in Iranian Kurdistan is patchy and demonstrates sharp variations from one region to another, even from one village to another.

With respect to the southern part of Iran, it is unclear how FGM appeared in this location. Some argue that the custom entered the country through a naval exchange between India and Somalia (Mohajer, 2010), and to this date some small communities of Afro Iranians live in Qeshm.

---

[11] In Chapter Three, an argument will be made for the legitimacy of the claim that FGM is not totally an Islamic belief, or more specifically that it should be associated only with the Shafi'i sect, because FGM is found neither in Kurdish Kermanji-speaking areas nor in large swathes within mainland Iranian Kurdistan where there has been no evidence of FGM for the last three generations.

In addition to southern parts of the nation, FGM exists in some villages and rural areas in Western Iran as well as in Kurdistan, Kermanshah and West Azerbaijan provinces.

In some venues girls are usually 'circumcised' between the ages of three and six with a sharp razor or a knife. Tradition then dictates that ash or cold water be applied to the wound. This is changing, however; increasingly, more hygienic materials such as Betadine and bandage pads are used.

Some locals in these parts, including Hormozgan province, believe that FGM came down to them from the Prophet Muhammad and that 'circumcised' women are purified. According to these believers, FGM keeps girls chaste by decreasing their sexual desire, preserving their virginity until marriage and producing faithful wives – rationalizations we have seen many times before.

Another local custom practiced in limited areas is *cheheltigh* (forty razors) believed to ablate girls' sexual urges, sweeten their aroma, and thereby increase their sexual allure for men. In the south and west of Iran, some *bibis* make a small razor cut in the thigh of the girl for parents who cannot bear to see their child suffer worse. This practice is called *Tighe Muhammedi* (Mohajer, 2010).

While *Tighe Muhammedi* and *cheheltigh* appear limited to Hormozgan province, beliefs elsewhere justify further varieties of 'surgery'. In various villages in Kermanshah and Kurdistan provinces, for instance, some women defend circumcising or at least cutting girls to rid them of dirty blood, even if only a small amount exits the child's body. Both religious and health reasons are given as motivating factors for this practice which locals call *Pajela*.

Similarly, some residents of Bandar Kong believe that women are evil creatures who can be saved from the reach of

Photo 9. Fieldwork, Mahabad-Bokau. (Credit: Kameel Ahmady)

the devil only by 'circumcision' (Jalali, 2007). In Bandar Kong, located five kilometers from Bandar Lengeh in the south of Iran, a shaving razor cuts the clitoris when infants are 40 days old or older. According to Parisa Rezazadeh Jalali's study, 70% of girls in this port city have been 'circumcised'.

As noted, faith plays a motivating role vis-à-vis FGM in Iran, as most groups that practice it call on religion to justify their actions. They usually believe that the rite emerged during the early years of the Islamic Kingdom and that the Prophet's and Imams' wives and daughters were 'circumcised'. (This is not, true, however; at least the Prophet's daughters and wife went genitally unscathed, but the belief, even if erroneous, motivates the cut to the present day.) Others argue it is both a religious duty and local tradition, and because their mothers and grandmothers did it they will continue. It should be acknowledged as well that most are unaware of FGM's medical consequences and health hazards (Jalali, 2007).

In sum, FGM remains a taboo issue in Iran even after the nation was included on the FGM-practicing list (Alawi and Schwartz, 2015). Government ministries either deny it exists or conceal its presence from the general population. A report from the Head of the Scientific Association of Social Workers of Iran stated that FGM, taking place in a limited number of villages with fewer than two thousand people, is mainly an African issue and not a serious problem. Although we lack reliable demographic surveys, research shows the numbers exceed this estimate.

Research Background

My enquiries began in 2005 when, for the first time after many years, I returned from Europe to my birthplace, Iranian Kurdistan, to find out more about FGM. Before that, I had been

Photo 10. Village of Hawraman, Marivan-Kurdistan. (Credit: Kameel Ahmady)

working in Africa for a number of humanitarian relief NGOs where I observed United Nations and UNICEF efforts in countries like Somalia, Kenya and Sudan to combat excision and infibulation.

Vague childhood memories surfaced, suggesting that FGM also existed in some parts of Iranian Kurdistan. This moved me to research the issue, starting with my own family and

Photo 11. Fieldwork in other provinces.
(Credit: Kameel Ahmady)

close relatives. I uncovered shocking evidence that FGM has long existed in areas of Mukriyan where I grew up and even in my own family. My grandmothers, mother and sister had been 'circumcised'.

Gradually, I began a field study and data collection in neighboring regions. The interviews and related footage became a film, at present the first and only publicly available documentary titled *In the Name of Tradition* about FGM in Iran.

Photo 12. Data collecting in the west of Iran.
(Credit: Kameel Ahmady)

It evolved from research in the Kurdish villages and neighborhoods of Mahabad, in additional villages in nearby Kurdistan
and in regions of Hawraman, located between the provinces
of Kurdistan and Kermanshah.[12]

Drawing on my training in social anthropology, I re-edited
the original documentary to accompany this study. It contains
footage of interviews from Kermanshah and Hormozgan, as
noted, and has been expanded with material from the provincial islands of Qeshm, Hormozgan and Kish. In addition to discussion with local women and *bibis*, the film records the
opinions of local men, medical staff, doctors, and clerics.

That further research is needed becomes evident in the film
as FGM had not yet been systematically investigated in Iran,
especially in geographical pockets of seemingly high prevalence. Thus, I launched a scientific nation-wide project.

---

[12] http://www.kameelahmady.com

Local resources were required to carry out such a comprehensive study. I therefore trained a number of young, enthusiastic male and female students and others willing to conduct most of the face-to-face interviews. Later, the research attracted more volunteers, and UNICEF-style standardized questionnaires were introduced to collect data. Strong communication and networking with the local population enabled my team and me to win their support as well as that of some community and religious leaders and a number of academics from civil society, both inside and outside Iran.

A lack of resources, funding, and legal authorization made it advisable to investigate in rural rather than in urban, cosmopolitan areas. Moreover, preliminary research and documentary evidence indicated that FGM is less likely to occur in towns, other than in outskirts and poor neighborhoods. Initially villages were picked at random from predefined geographical positions in the north, west, east, and south. However, as our inquiry progressed, we implemented more comprehensive village-by-village training and pilot projects, visiting an increasing number of locales in each state, taking samples, until we arrived in the southernmost province, Hormozgan, with the nation's highest rate of FGM.

Finding that Hormozgan housed the largest number of cut girls, our fact-finding mission and field work provided additional evidence of FGM in places such as Ilam, Lorestan, Chahar Mahaal and Bakhtiari, Kohgiluyeh and Boyer-Ahmad, Khuzestan, Bushehr, Sistan and Baluchestan, Golestan, Khorasne Shomali, Janobi and Razavi, Gilan, and in the more central parts of Iran such as Fars and Yezd.

The good news, however, concerns where it is NOT found. Despite the fact that some of these regions are home to a minority of Sunni Muslims, the study revealed, at times, no evidence of FGM. We can also confirm that the custom is foreign

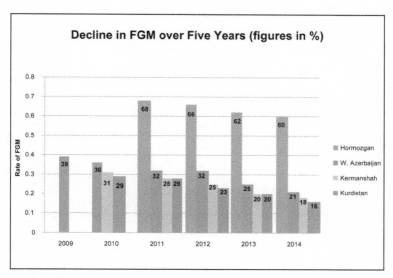

Figure 5. Decline in FGM over Five Years (figures in %)
(Credit: Kameel Ahmady)

to Sistan and Baluchistan despite a significant population of Sunni Muslims of the Hanafi sect (Hanafi is the *fiqh* with the largest number of Sunni Muslim). FGM is similarly absent among the forcibly migrated Kurds of Khorasan, Turkmens of Hanafi Muslim Golestan province, and among the small demographic of Turkish Sunni Shafi'i groups in Ardabil and West Azerbaijan provinces. Of further interest, the Sunni-populated areas of Larestan in Fars province, bordering Hormozgan, are also free of FGM, although some large Sunni areas of Hormozgan such as Bastak and its many villages do practice. Nonetheless, they cut at a much lower rate than in the same province in the more Southern regions and Islands.

Not unlike Larestan, for instance, in Khuzestan and Bushehr provinces, we found no cases of FGM among either Sunni Arabs or Shi'a Lur, though some evidence came to light among

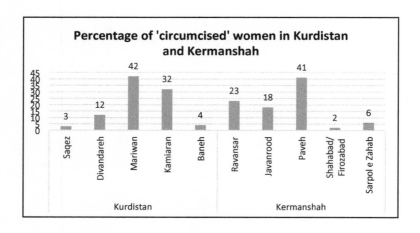

Figure 6. Percentage of excised women in Kurdistan and Kerman-shah (Credit: Kameel Ahmady)

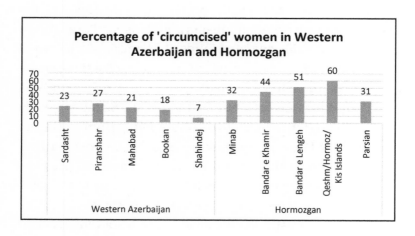

Figure 7. Percentage of excised women in Western Azerbaijan and Hormozgan (Credit: Kameel Ahmady)

old women in southern areas of Khuzestan. Genital cutting of girls was also absent from Lorstan, Chahar Mahaal and Bakhtiari provinces. In contrast, among Shi'a Kurds of Ilam and in villages near Mehran which neighbors Kermanshah, we uncovered very limited numbers amongst some elderly females above the age of 50. The study happily revealed that no young girls are being 'circumcised' now, which indicates a tradition fallen into desuetude in most Ilam and Kermanshah Shi'a communities.

Aided by maps, local guides, clerics and personal connections, a small but very enthusiastic group conducted research from 2005 to 2015. In some cases, bad road or weather conditions made it necessary to deviate from the scheduled route and to visit alternate locations. Since the study was not a full time project and was managed during different seasons, the initial fact-finding mission, field work and training spanned a decade.

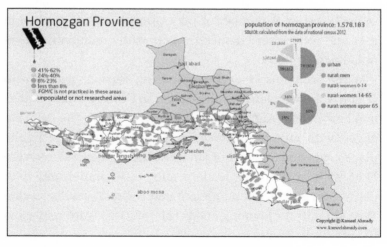

Figure 8. Prevalence of FGM in Hormozgan Province. (Credit: Kameel Ahmady)

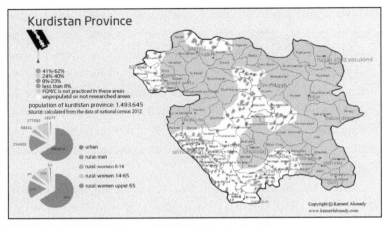

Figure 9. Prevalence of FGM in Kurdistan Province.
(Credit: Kameel Ahmady)

In addition to its longevity, the investigation also employed multiple approaches, strategies, methods, and tailor-made training manuals adapted to the various tastes and languages of each region. A number of pilot programs were applied in east and west where domestic visits with community stakeholders took place.

Mixed protocols in awareness-raising sessions mainly with young women highlighted the danger of FGM to female bodies and human life. And men, too, were sensitized. The team engaged with groups in mosques, private homes and public places, gauging its level of success. Lobbying sessions were held with community leaders and, most important, with clerics, local women, municipal and regional sheiks to gain their support for banning FGM. The religious were requested to issue local fatwas.

Each unit of fieldwork and face-to-face encounter entailed a second visit to the same village and then another trip one year later to assess the success and impact of the pilot programs.

More on Research Methodology

International data on FGM had been collected through a separate module of the Demographic and Health Surveys (DHS) Program since the beginning of 1990. The DHS has yielded a rich data set comparable over many countries, mainly in Africa. Since the prevalence of FGM in Iran had not been addressed by UNICEF or any other international organization, we decided to conduct the first ever country-wide data collection using a module resembling that of the DHS.

The sensitive subject matter influenced the methodology, primarily participatory. This framework privileged the views of women and girls, in particular those of victims, so that our findings would reflect their opinions. Interview questions were

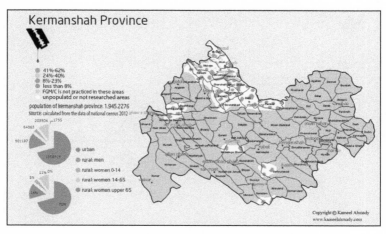

Figure 10. Prevalence of FGM in Kermanshah Province.
(Credit: Kameel Ahmady)

clear and 'user-friendly' to avoid any ambiguity or misunder-
standings between researchers and participants. Since the in-
vestigations stretched over a ten-year period, the approach
was adjusted along the way as we came up with new strategies.

Thus, as noted, using UNICEF-style standardized questionnaires, we collected data following the DHS model and
UNICEF's Multiple Indicator Cluster Surveys (MICS). Significantly, good communication and networking allowed our research teams to win indigenous support. Local people were
recruited to interview, and our training ensured ethical standards and confidentiality. I mean by 'ethics' what Tim May has
in mind. As May (1997) puts it, ethical standards "are binding,
hence need to be adhered to irrespective of the circumstances
surrounding the research; they remind us of our responsibilities to the people being researched" (2011, 54). He adds that it

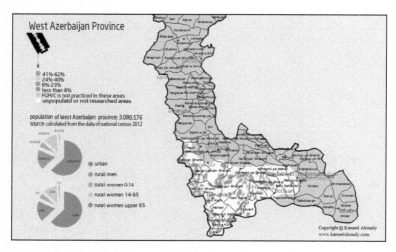

Figure 11. Prevalence of FGM in West Azerbaijan Province.
(Credit: Kameel Ahmady)

is also easier for participants if they can take part with peace of mind, having all relevant information about the destination of their input (May, 2011).

Given this good advice, we asked participants for their consent and informed them prior to the start of data collection how statements would be used and what our findings aimed to achieve. For the few telephone contacts, the same standards applied.

A total of 4000 interviews were carried out in the provinces of Hormozgan, West Azerbaijan, Kermanshah and Kurdistan. In each province, we talked to 1000 people, 750 women and 250 men. For the first time in iran, the male perspective was explored as well, to examine the role of fathers, husbands, and brothers in the perpetuation of FGM.

How Widespread is the Practice?

FGM occurs in some villages of one southern and three western provinces. The west is populated by a Sunni Shafi'i majority while the southern province, Hormozgan and its islands, is home to a significant Sunni Shafi'i community.

Given dispersal of religious and ethnic groups, mapping venues where genital cutting takes place is problematic and unlikely. For example, FGM as practiced in Iranian Kurdistan shows sharp variations from one region to another, even from one village to the next. In some cases, elements of the tradition are indisputable but in others, including adjacent settlements, the 'rite' has been in decline for the past two or three generations.

Changing times and modern life, the death and non-replacement of *bibis*, youth's lack of willingness to accept FGM, education, the impact of the media and some level of support from clerics are all factors in the declining rate. During the decade of this study, we observed the number of cases recede every year, for the reasons above and because of the training and awareness-raising campaigns that accompanied our research.

Refer to Figure 5, page 51 to see a reduction in FGM over the last five years.

Thus, we see FGM declining, albeit slowly, in part, I speculate, because even in Iran, only a limited number of people, all of whom belong to FGM-affected provinces, are aware of its existence within the country. The graph shows the slow pace of change during a six-year frame, starting with West Azerbaijan in 2009. During 2010, Kurdistan and Kermanshah also showed some decrease in the practice.

Sadly, however, Hormozgan, where prevalence is highest, maintained a rate of more than 60% at the end of 2014, while for the same period, we measured 21% in West Azerbaijan, 18% in Kermanshah, and 16% in Kurdistan. Nonetheless, the graph reveals that transformation has begun. The marked regions are responding to change.

The following section offers information on these four provinces.

Profiles of Selected Provinces

Hormozgan

In Hormozgan, population 1.5 million, we discovered that FGM is practiced on a massive number of baby girls in most Sunni Shafi'i villages. Also affected are enclaves in the town of Minab where some Shi'a families practice FGM; and villages and parts of the small towns Bandar Poal, Bandar Kong, Lengeh, Gavbandi (Persian) and Khamir. Genital cutting occurs as well on the minor islands of Hormuz and Larak. Qeshm, the largest island in the province, has a high number of victims among the mostly Sunni populations. And although it is home to large migrant groups of Shi'as from Minab, Bandar Abbass and other mainland Iranian towns who do not practice FGM, even on Kish Island, a tourist spot and one of Iran's wealthiest places, girls are cut, commonly undergoing Type I which our data shows is most common in this province. Homa Ahadi's research on prevalence in Hormozgan notes that, of the 400 interviews she conducted, 87.4% had Type I (Ahadi et al., 2009). She also claims to have found some type 2, but this study cannot confirm cases of FGM type 2 or worse.

United Arab Emirates (UAE)

Because local people have families in the Gulf region and other nearby countries, it is likely that FGM occurs in the Gulf. Interviews with locals from the South (dual nationals or immigrants) and findings from limited field work in the UAE confirm that daughters in immigrant Muslim families in the United Arab Emirates suffer genital abuse including groups from Iran, Oman, Yemen, and Bahrain. Most neighborhoods have their own *bibis* and many families plan to 'circumcise' offspring while visiting their home countries.

In addition, confirmed cases of FGM have been found in some neighborhoods of Shehba, Noof and Garain in Sharjah; Sherisha and Jolan in Ras Al Khaima and in Satwa, Dubai. These communities have their own local practitioners. At the time of this study, two *bibis* in Noof as well as one *bibi* and two family *bibis* in Jolan still inflict FGM.

See Figures 6 and 7, page 52, for the prevalence of genital cutting.

Kurdistan

In Kurdistan, population 1.3 million, the majority practice Sunni Islam with a Shi'a minority of Kurds and Turks residing in Qorveh and Bijar. The main language, Kurdish, is heard in various dialects of which Sorani/Ardalani is most common; Kalhori and Hawramani can be found as well.[13] Concerning FGM, Kurdistan, together with Kermanshah, is the province in the west of Iran with the largest number of cut girls. Some villages in Mariwan and especially Hawraman Tekht (in Upper Hawraman region) have high rates of vulva abuse, likely resulting from proximity to Kermanshah province's victims. Villages in Hawraman Tekht, recently declared districts, have the highest rates in both Hawraman areas, divided between the two provinces of Kermanshah and Kurdistan. Additional villages such as Kemalle and Belber, a number of towns in Sandenj Kamyaran, and enclaves in Saqqez and Bana, however, do not cut female genitals; inhabitants confirm that for decades they have not heard of a single case.

Kermanshah

Kermanshah province, population 1.8 million, is divided among groups belonging to the Shi'a and Sunni Shafi'i branches of Islam with, among others, a large minority of Ahel Haq and Lak plus a small number of Bahai. The main languages spoken in Kermanshah are Kurdish (Jaff, Feyli and Kalhori), Hawramani, Laki and Persian. FGM is found mainly in the area called Hawraman with part of the Hawraman region located in neighboring Kurdistan province and in the region of the Jaff tribe, also named after a dialect. Various villages belonging to Kamyarn, Ravansar, Jevanrod, Pava, Nodsha, Nosod (Mansoor Agai) are the most affected in Kermanshah province.

The incidence of FGM among young women is, however, considerably lower in Kermanshah than other provinces we studied; and the same applies for Kamyarn and Pava, though not in all villages. At least in some of the above districts evi-

---

[13] Some Hawramanis believe, however, that their language and ethnicity are independent of Kurdish.

dence shows that people abandoned the practice decades ago. Children and juveniles are less likely to be cut, but among women older than 30 to 35 the rate increases, reaching its highest point among the over-50s. It is important nonetheless to recognize that the low rate among juveniles may also be caused by the custom of cutting at more advanced ages. In other places, late mutilations are marginal.

West Azerbaijan
In West Azerbaijan, population 3 million, the Kurdish peoples reside mainly in the southern part of the province; however, a minority of Kermanji-speaking Kurds also live near the border with Turkey, from Uromiya to the town of Mako.

Field research indicates that the number of elderly women who have undergone FGM is alarmingly high; and in complete contrast, the rate of FGM among children is very low and declining every year. The study found that in some villages of the Mokrian region, few girls younger than 10 have been cut. One reason for this diminishing rate in the south of West Azerbaijan relates to the seasonal illegal crossing of Roma (gypsies known locally as Dom or Gerechi) from Iraqi Kurdistan into Iranian Kurdistan.

These groups increase their income by carrying out FGM. The majority abjure safe methods, and a serious risk of disease and disability results. Years of monitoring genital cutting along the border with Iraq found that most of West Azerbaijan province and villages near the frontier depend on Iraqi Kurdish Roma groups to mutilate their daughters. The tightening of border security by the Iranian guards and the regional conflict within Iraq means that fewer contingents manage to cross illegally, which has reduced the rate of FGM in this particular province.

However, unlike West Azerbaijan, Kurdistan and Kermanshah rely on their own *bibis* and self-trained old women to keep the tradition alive.

The rest of this study offers an overview of FGM from multiple perspectives.

Prevalence of FGM by Age

Figures 12-17, pages 78 - 80, give an overview of 'circumcised' women by age in four provinces. For uniformity in result, an equal number of villages per province were chosen for research. The results clearly demonstrate regional differences in prevalence.

Figure 15, page 79, reveals the high percentage of cut women in some villages in Hormozgan province, where the rate can reach 60%, and in some villages of Qeshm, Hormuz and Larak islands. Prevalence is lowest in some ethnic Parsian villages, at 31%; northern parts of the province were FGM free.

Kermanshah province, figure 13, page 78, had the second-highest prevalence at 42% in some villages of Marivan. However, in Kermanshah the rates are more modest, and in West Azerbaijan, figure 14, page 79, the numbers are comparatively lower still.

Analysis shows that the proportion of 'circumcised' women in the 30-49 age bracket is higher than among women and girls aged 15 to 29. In some villages of Hormozgan and Qeshm Island, up to 61% of women aged 29 to 49 had been harmed; in contrast, cutting appears to have ended in Lakastan in Kermanshah, where this study uncovered no evidence of it among women and girls aged 15 to 29.

These findings therefore demonstrate an encouraging trend: FGM is decreasing in all four provinces. For instance, in

Piranshahr, West Azerbaijan, the rate is less than 10% among the youth. Similarly, in Javanrood in the same province, we see a sharp decline from 41% in older women to 9% in teens, adolescents and girls. In some of the villages of Ravansar, it has again decreased dramatically, falling to 17% from 43%.

From the inverse relationship between age and prevalence, we can infer that women who have been 'circumcised' know the suffering this practice brings. Our feedback suggested the new generation's awareness and determination to lead their own lives. Therefore, when a couple marries, they prefer to spare their daughters the pain that tradition forced their grandmothers to bear.

Precise questioning permitted us to calculate the proportion of 'circumcised' women by age. We also wanted to uncover attitudinal changes of mothers towards genital cutting. The survey assures us that an increasing number hope to end it.

Figures 18 - 21, page 81 - 82, show the ratio of women who have undergone FGM aged 15 - 49 with at least one daughter subjected to clitoridectomy. The difference among the 15 - 29 and 30 - 49 brackets is prominent in Kermanshah, where we see a decline exceeding 90% in Javanrood and Ravansar, with around 50% in Paveh and no evidence of FGM among those 15 - 29 in the Lakastan area. The same applies in Sarpol e Zahab. In Hormozgan province, the number of wounded has been cut nearly in half; in West Azerbaijan, a 90% difference between generations is recorded. Kurdistan also mirrors Hormozgan with a fall in excess of 90% in some areas.

Now, a caveat adheres to this encouraging story of decline. The data reflect those mothers who had the opportunity to 'circumcise' their daughters but refused. A large number mentioned, however, that their other daughters are still too young. Once they reach an appropriate age, they will undergo FGM.

Impact of Education

Following DHS and MICS guidelines, we collected data on the educational attainment of mothers, focusing on the relationship between schooling and FGM rates in their daughters.

Figures 22 - 25, pages 83 - 84, reveal a significant impact of education. According to the findings, a woman's years in the classroom are among the most important influences on the outcome for her daughter. The research indicates that female

Photo 13. Most men are aware of FGM. (Credit: Shirin Talandeh)

graduates prefer to release their child from a harmful custom. Conversely, the lower the amount of schooling, the more likely a mother is to follow tradition, considering it a social norm or religious duty.

Nonetheless, a few of the high school and university-educated had one of their daughters cut. The rate, however, is either vanishingly small in the four provinces, or non-existent, i.e. no case at all surfaced among women with advanced degrees. The data collected from the Kurdish region suggest, therefore, that, due to women's increasingly high educational attainment, the practice is in decline.

The findings also show that the university educated are less likely to support FGM generally, with fewer than 20% of those surveyed doing so. However, for such attitudes to make a practical difference, these same women must be empowered.

Photo 14. Women with no FGM in Basher.
(Credit: Kameel Ahmady)

Impact of Religion

Our research confirmed the findings of previous studies: FGM is a ritual performed mainly by Sunnis in Iran. Whereas much of the world considers genital cutting an Islamic practice, this is in error, contention in theological opinion notwithstanding. Shias, who make up the Iranian majority, see FGM as a tradition related to the Sunni sect; they do not consider its performance a religious but rather an ethnic obligation. Therefore, the prevalence of FGM is strikingly low in the Shia population. Yet it exists.

For the most part, however, our research uncovered a striking difference in FGM prevalence amongst Shia populations compared to their Sunni counterparts, especially in Kurdistan where Shias do not practice FGM, and in West Azerbaijan where only 2% of Shi'as do, with those few who cut residing in Shahindej villages. In Lakastan and Sarpol e Zahab villages, the rates among Shia are 4% and 5% respectively. In Hormozgan province, moreover, some evidence of FGM in Shia communities has been recorded in selected villages, showing that though rare, genital abuse continues there.

See figures 25 - 26, pages 84 - 85.

Impact of Household Wealth

Poverty also plays a role in the prevalence of FGM in Iran. Financial status can influence decisions to cut. To measure the impact of income, DHS and MICS questionnaires gathered information on household assets and home ownership along with characteristics of dwellings such as available sanitation facilities and access to safe drinking water.

We weighted each asset (factor) and ranked individuals according to the total score of the household in which they reside. See figures 27 - 30, pages 85 - 87.

Photo 15. Woman from Minab on Qeshm Island.
(Credit: Shirin Talandeh)

Photo 16. Women less likely to have undergone FGM in West Azerbaijan province. (Credit: Kameel Ahmady)

Overall, even if the relationship between wealth and genital cutting is not always consistent, totals appear to drop among women from affluent families so that, in general, well-to-do daughters are more likely to grow up intact. In our four provinces excision affected less than 15% of richer women.

Further, the venues we studied were homogeneous in terms of FGM prevalence among wealthy homesteads. Only in a few Mariwan villages in Kurdistan and Paveh villages in Kermanshah were the rates higher, at 23% and 19% respectively, while the rest held steady at 15%. But this is really not surprising. Improved financial status allows access to a better life, education, exposure, and knowledge; therefore, wives and mothers from the more leisured classes assess their options differently. Nonetheless, some among the affluent adhere to FGM.

Men and Women's Perceptions of FGM

To better understand why FGM continues, we aimed to uncover how gendered perceptions of the phenomenon influence its survival and to find out who holds the decision-making power. Our questionnaires focused on men's and women's differences.

The data reveal that the most prominent figures in determining whether a girl is subject to FGM are female, mostly mothers or grandmothers, but sometimes another female relative; men have some say but not a central one.

Regarding support for the custom, the figures 31 - 32, pages 87 - 88, show that in Hormozgan 44% of women approve it in Qeshm, Hormuz and Larak islands while the corresponding level among men is 33%. In Paveh and Javanrood in Kermanshah backing is lower, at 21% of women and fewer than 10% of men. The results suggest that despite the patriarchal nature of society, men appear less concerned with FGM than women. Women, however, responding to the silent pressure of the patriarchy, feel compelled to continue cutting.

Types of FGM Practitioner

Another factor perpetuating FGM is some cutters' vested interests. Their earnings from *sunnet* may be either their only source of income or represent a substantial percentage. This observation applies to Roma groups, *bibis* and family members (in practice, older women).

However, the scenario in every province is unique. In Hormozgan, *bibis* are the most likely cutters; in some areas or situations, however, family members may be involved. In West Azerbaijan, in contrast, FGM is primarily an activity for Roma groups without passports or visas who cross illegally from Iraqi Kurdistan into West Azerbaijan, gambling with arrest by Iranian border police. Despite most Roma practitioners' unhygienic 'surgical' procedures, they earn a good income from FGM.

In addition to the Roma, a mixed cohort of family members and traditional practitioners was also found, the latter most frequent in Kermanshah and Kurdistan villages although Roma and *bibis* are not wholly absent. The former perform FGM with a razor, thorn, or knife, without anesthesia; medicalized or hygienic 'circumcision' is unknown.

See figures 33 - 38, pages 88 - 91.

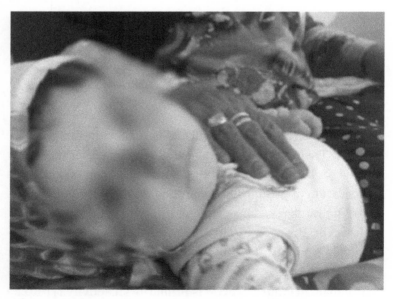

Photo 17. Four month old after FGM. (Credit: Kameel Ahmady)

Photo 18. Pir Shalyar, Hawraman religious site.
(Credit: Kameel Ahmady)

Educated Women Who Support FGM

As we have seen, the indisputable importance of learning in shaping opinion led us to examine how levels of schooling influenced support for FGM in the selected provinces. Although the ratio of educated women favoring FGM is relatively high in Hormozgan province, it falls to between 11% to 19% elsewhere.

Similarly, in West Azerbaijan, well-informed women's esteem for the practice is low, as it is in Kermanshah where female respondents with some years of schooling oppose it by 6%, 7%, and 18% in Javanrood, Ravansar, and Paveh villages, respectively. Kurdistan compares favorably: although a small contingent of knowledgeable interviewees still back genital maiming, a far greater number oppose it. Clearly, education can be deployed to influence viewpoints and behavior. Additional prerequisites of female empowerment, however, can also make a difference.

See figures 39 - 42, pages 91 - 93.

Summary of Findings

Most research ended in 2014 and, despite a few setbacks, much had been achieved over a decade that included travelling thousands of kilometers, visiting more than 200 villages and interviewing over 4,000 women and some men from different areas and social classes in search of comprehensive data about FGM in Iran. Although not yet having been fully evaluated, preliminary findings demonstrate that the practice is widespread in certain villages (affecting around 60% of females in some venues in Qeshm Island for example), and is especially grave in settlements in four provinces in the northwest, west and south of Iran. Of equal interest is its absence in proximate settings. We uncovered no cases in the northern parts of West Azerbaijan where people are Kurmanji Kurdish speakers, nor did it appear in southern Kermanshah or northern Hormozgan.

The most accurate estimate of the rate of FGM today must be inferred from the number of newborns and young children currently being mutilated. It is a good sign that the percentage among women and girls aged 15 to 29 is lower by 30% in comparison with women aged 30 to 49, and it descends to less than 8% among children below the age of 10. These points lead us to conclude that the number of cases has fallen steadily in the last few decades.

This success notwithstanding, interviews with citizens of both sexes aged 15 to 49 indicate that 38% still support genital cutting for reasons of religion, tradition and culture. Thus, to reach zero tolerance, immediate intervention and awareness programs together with public engagement projects are urgently required.

And there's another caveat. Even if support among younger generations is lower, and FGM rates have declined in each of the past 10 years, the speed of change remains sluggish. The important factors in decline all relate to what we might term "modernity"; better access to education; lack of interest in religion among youth; ease of entry to various media, partly through the advances of technology; and the impact of migration from villages to towns (a large number of villagers have a secondary home in a nearby town). What is more, elderly *bibis* no longer able to travel are not being replaced by younger apprentices.

How have these conclusions been reached? Our research employed mixed techniques. Interviews comprised both open-ended and closed questions, and the figures reflect a mix of qualitative and quantitative methods. For this reason, the raw data is suggestive but cannot give a wholly accurate picture of reality on the ground.

Likewise, when trying to assess the impact of any intervention, we found that the complexity cannot be captured by a single evaluative procedure. Mixed methods combining apparent and hidden realities with the outcomes of qualitative and quantitative methodology produce a comprehensive analysis of the problem (Bamberger, 2000). An example would be the higher percentage of women who, compared to their male counterparts, support FGM and are most responsible for imposing it. Why? Our questionnaire elicited the following explanation from these women: because a girl's virginity is of vital importance to secure her future and marital status, they said, she is obliged to protect it by any means possible. Failure means she has ruined her family's honor. To relieve her of this heavy burden and preserve the reputation of her kin by any means, women continue the ritual of 'circumcision'.

The Pilot Interventions

Following the initial data collection, we launched pilot projects in 2010 to examine locally modified means to reduce FGM in parts of Iran – the Persian and Arab regions in the south and the Kurdish area in the west.

We assumed that certain well-defined, low profile interventions can accelerate abandonment in contrast to forced cessation by government or other powers outside the community. This study, grounded in Iranian traditions and culture, adopted a holistic, culturally sensitive, participatory approach based on a firm foundation of human rights.

Projects were divided into two categories: one focused on the community, the second enabled advocacy and networking. Concentrating on the grassroots means designing diplomatic interventions that will work to prevent FGM and these in turn require indirectness, since any straight-forward effort to outlaw the custom could sabotage the entire research project, deeply anchored as tradition is. The second category permitted us to engage with the local people in an even less confrontational way.

Because this was a pilot project, resources were limited, yet despite budgetary constraints, we secured the services of certified local professionals – one social worker, one psychologist, and one nurse. To maximize cooperation and gain trust from neighborhood men and women, interviewers and interviewees shared the same ethnicity. To obtain better coverage, our staff were trained to undertake field work on their own. Once they had mapped their territories and begun to function independently, they used social events as platforms, attending weddings, *Quran* lessons and funerals. This strategy improved and increased access to the public.

The pilot intervention supported the findings of the research as a whole, that FGM is widespread in some areas while declining in others. Following the initial effort, the focus gradually shifted from providing medical advice and care to promoting FGM awareness through teaching, lobbying and networking with stakeholders, community leaders, and prominent clerics.

Although budget and time limitations prevented full assessment of the pilot study, our efforts bore fruit. They are instructive and replicable.

STATISTICS

On the following pages, you will find the graphic material to accompany the preceeding narratives.

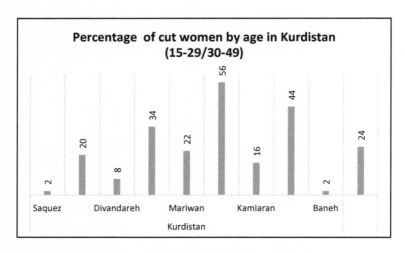

Figure 12. Percentage of cut women by age in Kurdistan.
(Credit: Kameel Ahmady).

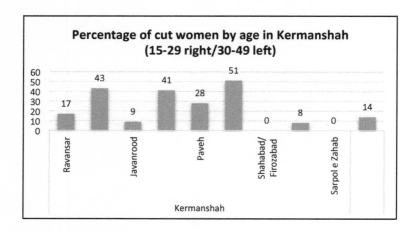

Figure 13. Percentage of cut women by age in Kermanshah.
(Credit: Kameel Ahmady).

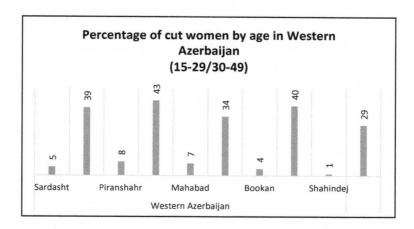

Figure 14. Percentage of cut women by age in Western Azerbaijan. (Credit: Kameel Ahmady).

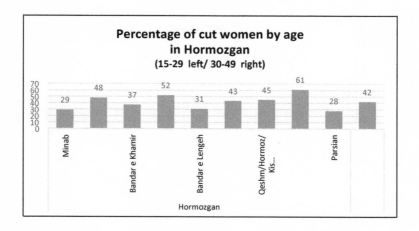

Figure 15. Percentage of cut women by age in Hormozgan. (Credit: Kameel Ahmady).

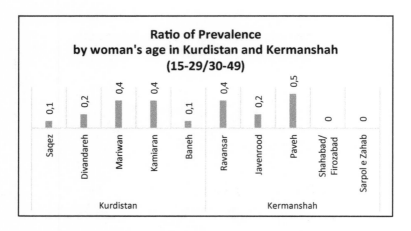

Figure 16. Ratio of prevalence by woman's age in Kurdistan and Kermanshah. (Credit: Kameel Ahmady)

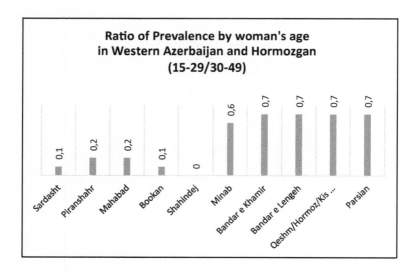

Figure 17. Ratio of prevalence by woman's age in Western Azerbaijan and Hormozgan. (Credit: Kameel Ahmady)

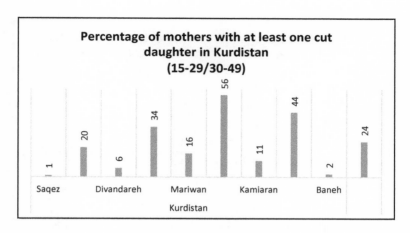

Figure 18. Percentage of mothers with at least one cut daughter in Kurdistan. (Credit: Kameel Ahmady)

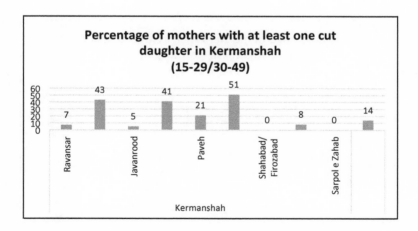

Figure 19. Percentage of mothers with at least one cut daughter in Kermanshah. (Credit: Kameel Ahmady)

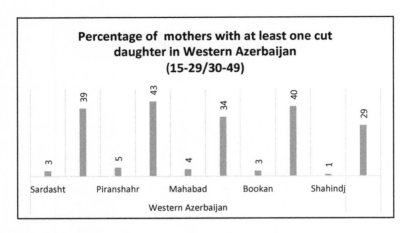

Figure 20. Percentage of mothers with at least one cut daughter in Western Azerbaijan. (Credit: Kameel Ahmady)

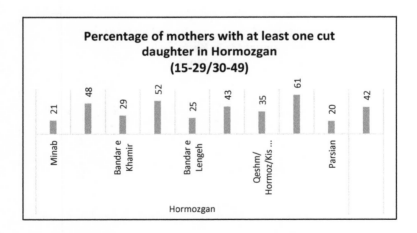

Figure 21. Percentage of mothers with at least one cut daughter in Hormozgan. (Credit: Kameel Ahmady)

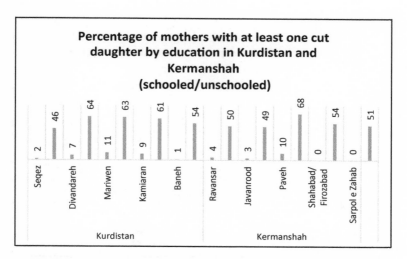

Figure 22. Percentage of mothers with at least one cut daughter, by education, in Kurdistan and Kermanshah. (Credit: Kameel Ahmady)

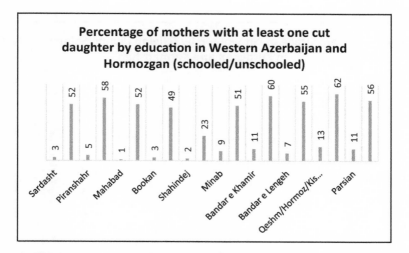

Figure 23. Percentage of mothers with at least one cut daughter, by education, in Western Azerbaijan and Hormozgan. (Credit: Kameel Ahmady)

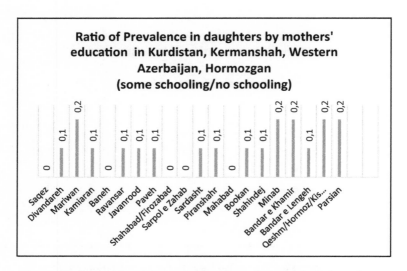

Figure 24. Ratio of prevalence in daughters by mothers' education (some schooling/no schooling). (Credit: Kameel Ahmady)

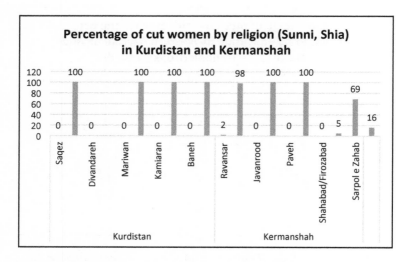

Figure 25. Percentage of cut women by religion (Sunni, Shia) in Kurdistan and Kermanshah. (Credit: Kameel Ahmady)

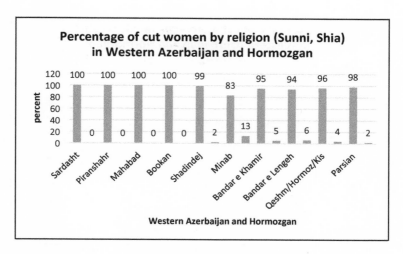

Figure 26. Percentage of cut women by religion (Sunni, Shia) in Western Azerbaijan and Hormozgan. (Credit: Kameel Ahmady)

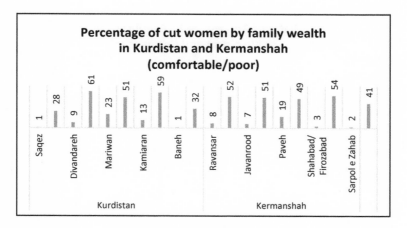

Figure 27. Percentage of cut women by family wealth in Kurdistan and Kermanshah (comfortable/poor). (Credit: Kameel Ahmady)

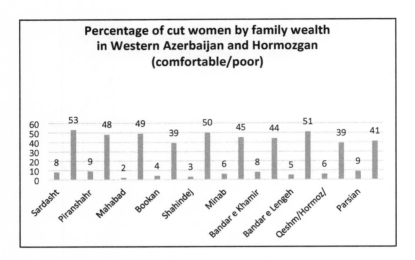

Figure 28. Percentage of cut women by family wealth in Western Azerbaijan and Hormozgan (comfortable/poor). (Credit: Kameel Ahmady)

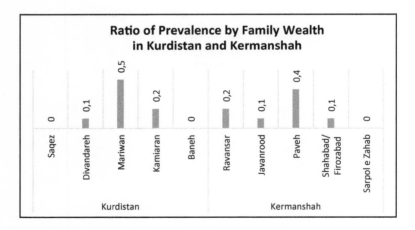

Figure 29. Ratio of prevalence by family wealth in Kurdistan and Kermanshah. (Credit: Kameel Ahmady)

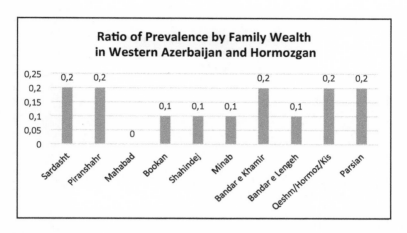

Figure 30. Ratio of prevalence by family wealth in Western Azerbaijan and Hormozgan. (Credit: Kameel Ahmady)

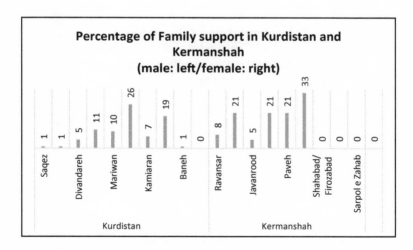

Figure 31. Percentage of family support in Kurdistan and Kermanshah. (Credit: Kameel Ahmady)

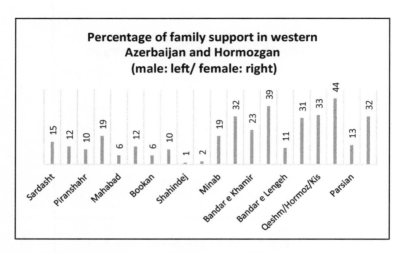

Figure 32. Percentage of family support in Western Azerbaijan and Hormozgan. (Credit: Kameel Ahmady)

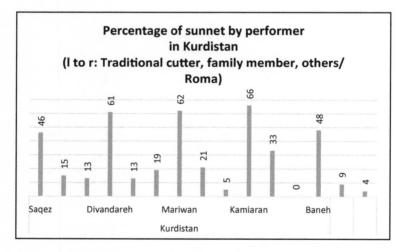

Figure 33. Percentage of sunnet by performer in Kurdistan. (Credit: Kameel Ahmady)

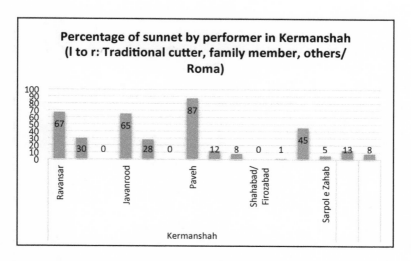

Figure 34. Percentage of sunnet by performer in Kermanshah. (Credit: Kameel Ahmady)

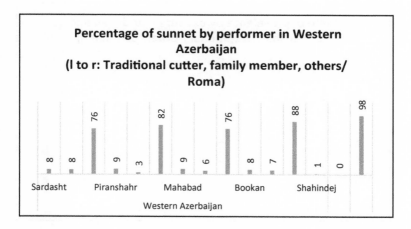

Figure 35. Percentage of sunnet by performer in Western Azerbaijan. (Credit: Kameel Ahmady)

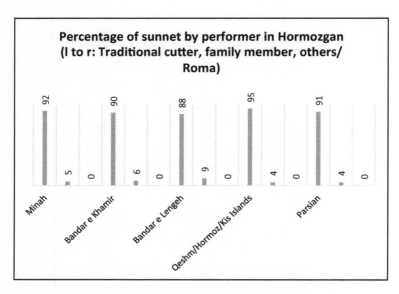

*Figure 36. Percentage of sunnet by performer in Hormozgan.
(Credit: Kameel Ahmady)*

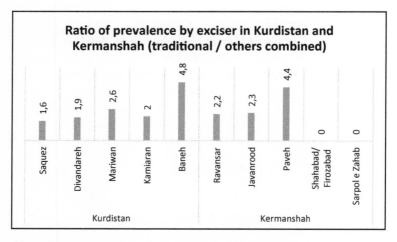

*Figure 37. Ratio of prevalence by exciser in Kurdistan and
Kermanshah. (Credit: Kameel Ahmady)*

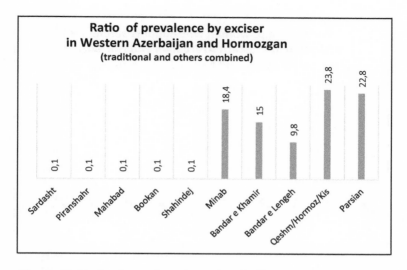

Figure 38. Ratio of prevalence by exciser in Western Azerbaijan and Hormozgan. (Credit: Kameel Ahmady)

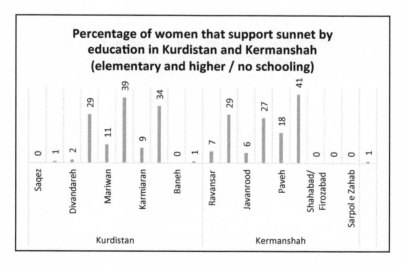

Figure 39. Percentage of women who support sunnet by education in Kurdistan and Kermanshah. (Credit: Kameel Ahmady)

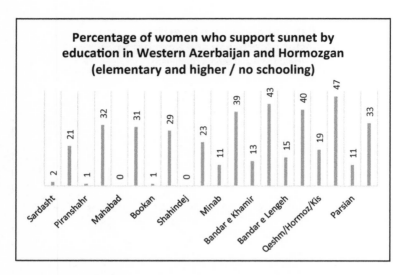

Figure 40. Percentage of women who support sunnet by education in Western Azerbaijan and Hormozgan. (Credit: Kameel Ahmady)

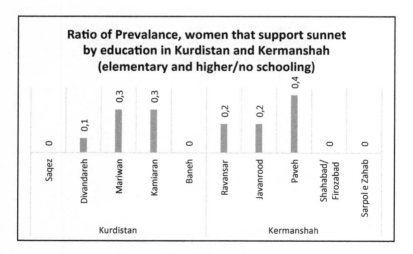

Figure 41. Ratio of prevalence among women who support FGM in Kurdistan and Kermanshah. (Credit: Kameel Ahmady)

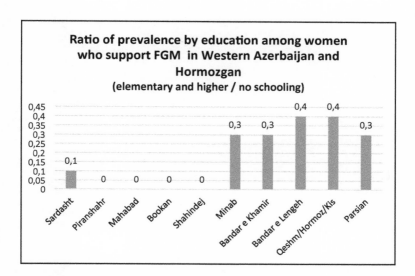

Figure 42. Ratio of prevalence by education among women who support FGM in Western Azerbaijan and Hormozgan. (Credit: Kameel Ahmady)

CHAPTER THREE

Fight against FGM. A Historical Perspective & Present-day Scenario

To date, we have indeed made progress toward overcoming FGM, but, since the start of the new millennium, only with substantial effort; we still have some distance to go. This chapter puts the fight against FGM in historical perspective to examine where we are today in light of where we were. It elaborates on international laws against the practice, considers their weaknesses, and looks at discussions on genital ablation being waged among prominent Muslim clerics who have issued fatwas on the topic. Finally, we turn to major opponents, including the Iranian government itself, to assess how it is handling its responsibilities and obligations.

Historical Overview of the Fight against FGM

Available documentation confirms that efforts to combat FGM began in Africa in the early 20th century, although the undocumented history of this struggle by local people may be even older. The arrival of European colonial administrators and Western missionaries ignited a debate about banning female 'circumcision'. Christian clerics objected to the practice as a violation of religious principles, but their attempts to eliminate it failed. These setbacks notwithstanding, post-colonial regimes passed many laws against FGM, but half-hearted enforcement of the legislation that had been based on ineffective information miscarried as well.

One highlight among these early efforts took place in 1929 after the Kenya Missionary Council began referring to female 'circumcision' as 'female genital mutilation'. Hulda Stumpf, an American missionary and strong opponent of FGM, was murdered after being 'circumcised' (Robert, 1996).

Fast forward to the 1960s and '70s. Women's groups raised their voices against the custom through massive campaigns and rallies. These decades also marked the start of resistance from health professionals in FGM-practicing countries whose medical journal articles shaped opinions. Their objections lay in personal observation of clinical complications. In 1979, the first global seminar on the subject, sponsored by the Eastern Regional section of the World Health Organization (WHO), focused on the findings of an Austrian-American journalist and Harvard-trained city planner, Fran Hosken (1920-2006) who had researched the subject in Africa and had been invited as the keynote speaker. Her insistence on the need to stop all forms of harmful traditional practices was well-received by seminar participants, but soon thereafter, in the summer of 1980 at the UN Mid-Decade for Women Conference in Copen-

United Nations Entity for Gender Equality and the Empowerment of Women

hagen, her efforts generated considerable controversy and her intervention was rejected. So the issue remained unresolved. However, Hosken's action was the first to open up an international platform for negotiation around FGM.

Since then worldwide efforts to convince experts that genital ablation should be stopped culminated in recognition of FGM as a human rights violation by the United Nations General Assembly on 20 December 2012. Initially, campaigns had stressed the physical harm caused by amputation of body parts. In the 1980s, however, FGM came to be discussed as a human rights issue, with the gender lens enhanced during the 1990s as the slogan "women's rights are human rights" gained popularity.

Awareness-raising to prevent violence against women lent campaigns against genital mutilation their international edge, encouraging legislation to outlaw the practice. The decade also supported numerous international colloquia placing FGM within human rights work: the World Conference on Human Rights in Vienna in 1993, the International Conference on Population and Development (ICPD) in Cairo in 1994, and the Fourth World Conference on Women in Beijing (Beijing Conference) in 1995 are especially prominent, leading to the aforementioned UN General Assembly vote in 2012 initiated by the African Group with support from No Peace Without Justice. In this regard, Khady Koita deserves special mention. Twice invited to address the UN, she became the poster child for abolition.[14]

In addition to governmental efforts, African women like Khady, authentic witnesses to what they call 'torture', have also fought to abolish FGM. Even after recriminations that had

---

[14] For further details see Khady's memoir, *Blood Stains. A Child of Africa Reclaims Her Human Rights*. Trans. Tobe Levin. Frankfurt am Main: UnCUT/Voices Press, 2010

been hurled at Western activists in Copenhagen sabotaged nascent alliances on which solid funding depended, these immigrant pioneers continued, founding effective NGOs. For instance, Efua Dorkenoo OBE from Ghana launched FORWARD in the UK in 1983; even earlier, in the late 70s, Awa Thiam from Senegal started CAMS in Paris, and both associations continue as strong lobbyists to this day.

Shortly thereafter, in 1984, a strengthened movement in African hands emerged. The Inter-African Committee on Traditional Practices affecting the Health of Women and Children (IAC) was founded in Dakar, Senegal. It now operates in 29 African countries and 19 affiliated branches in the world to educate national governments and civil society about the evils of genital ablation.

The African women's struggle proved immensely productive, and in February 2003, the IAC conference in Addis Ababa, Ethiopia, declared 6 February an "International Day of Zero Tolerance to FGM." The following year UNICEF's Innocenti Research Centre published a seminal report entitled *Changing a Harmful Social Convention: Female Genital Mutilation/ Cutting* which in turn provoked a response in the Bamako Declaration.[15]

In recent years, efforts against FGM have focused more on raising awareness through information, education and communication campaigns. To reach the broadest public, artistic methods, such as music, theater and film, are also in abundant use. In addition, the health sector, together with legal and human rights organizations, is proactive and has included information on FGM in training programs on women's rights for lawyers, judges and society at large.

One of the most significant recent events, inspired by the late Efua Dorkenoo OBE, is joint sponsorship by the UK government and UNICEF of the first international Girl Summit conference in July 2014 (RCW, 2014). Aimed primarily at ending child marriage and FGM, it brought together officials from affected nations and high-income countries, community leaders, the private sector and figures from the media. The gathering hoped to mobilize political will, ensure governments and communities commit to barring FGM, and guarantee adequate funding. One highlight was a pledge to abrogate the sense of social obligation to amputate girls' genitals. The conference concluded with the commitment by 21 nations to join a global abolition movement. Follow-up would be assured by the UK government's Department for International Development

---

[15] http://nofgm.org/2014/11/12/the-bamako-declaration-female-genital-mutilation-terminology-mali-2005/. Accessed 2 May 2016.

Photo 19. Bandar Lengeh. (Credit: Kameel Ahmady)

(DfID) whose team will monitor performance of obligations taken on during the conference.

International Laws

With gradual recognition of FGM as a violation of human rights, a worldwide campaign began urging implementation of laws against it. Committed to protecting the rights of women and children, many countries have ratified international and regional treaties addressing various forms of discrimination and violence. For example, FGM is now illegal in at least 17 out of 28 FGM-practicing nations including Burkina Faso, Senegal, Côte d'Ivoire, Ghana, Djibouti, Guinea, Togo, Tanzania, Kenya, the Central African Republic and Egypt. In addition,

Senegal, Sudan, Egypt and Ethiopia have named genital excision a crime. Most European governments receiving immigrants from regions that cut have also passed legislation; some, like the UK, Sweden, Norway and Belgium enacted specific laws to punish the practice whereas others, like France, address FGM under general criminal codes. Moreover, in 2011, the Spanish regime began to prosecute immigrant families taking daughters to countries of origin for FGM. In early 2015, Spanish medical specialists proposed requiring examinations and, as in the Netherlands, having the foreign-born sign declarations not to harm their daughters' genitalia when they visit their ancestral homes.

The Weakness of Law against FGM in the Middle East and Iran

The President of the Iranian Association of Social Workers contends that "female 'circumcision' is absent from ancient Persia," admitting, however, that if "we find the crime committed against Iranian girls [it takes place only] in some villages and remote parts of the country." The operation, Jahan notes, is sometimes justified as an explicit attempt to decrease a girl's sexual stimulation while, in his view, it remains rare in the nation as a whole, restricted to a few locales with populations under two thousand. In fact, the Social Workers' chief hopes to divert attention from the issue in Iran altogether: "This intervention happens mostly in African countries. Neighboring nations also practice it to some extent but its center is in Africa."

My research suggests otherwise. Even in Iran, the centuries-old practice of *sunnet* is so strongly embedded in community norms that enforcing new criminal legislation remains challenging, even if explicit paragraphs are inserted into existing penal codes. As long as talking about FGM is taboo in the Middle East, its reality will be denied and enforcement made especially difficult. Nonetheless, some government action against genital ablation can be noted. For example, Iraq has enacted a law to tackle FGM, especially in the south of Iraqi Kurdistan, and jurisprudence has begun to bear fruit despite minimal results early on. After all, a dismal rate of change is actually the norm. Look at Egypt: with FGM affecting more than four out of five females, practitioners flaunt the law to continue with impunity, and the 'Arab Spring', which could have given this abuse of women a higher profile, has been, on the whole, disappointing.

Thus, in Iran, lack of support makes any action against FGM especially taxing. Neither government nor NGOs have proven helpful. After all, Iran refused to ratify the Convention on the Elimination of All Forms of Discrimination against Women even though President Muhammad Khatami's Parliament approved joining CEDAW. Sadly, Iran's powerful Guardian Council vetoed the legislation – for contradicting Islamic principles.

Nevertheless, the nation's legal system can prosecute and punish mutilation of the body. Relevant documents include, for instance, the Women's Responsibilities and Entitlement Charters on the right to life and physical integrity; the right to protection against victimization, the right to mental and physical health and the right to be free of family violence. Still, since enforcement is patchy, successful claims by FGM victims are rare. Moreover, since no legislation specifically mentions genital offense, the Islamic law of Iran does not protect females from it (Alawi and Schwartz, 2015). This failure to safeguard means that lay midwives – not medical professionals – are enabled to perform the cutting in people's homes. The secretive nature of these assaults thus increases women's health risks. Lack of information coupled with government denial keeps the issue under the radar of relevant ministries' attention (Alawi and Schwartz, 2015).

These hurdles notwithstanding, Iran has strengthened its penal code by adding general anti-mutilation laws. Articles 479 and 663 of the Islamic Penal Code allow invoking *qisas* when the cutting of female genital organs is detected. Mutilated persons can also look to the Iranian Protection Law for People with Disabilities enacted in 2003 and the Convention on the Rights of Persons with Disabilities, in force since 2007.

Iran has also ratified the Convention on the Rights of the Child (CRC). Article 2 paragraph 2 notes that "States Parties shall take all appropriate measures to ensure that the child is protected against all forms of discrimination or punishment on the basis of the status, activities, expressed opinions, or beliefs of the child's parents, legal guardians, or family members."

Photo 20. A village in Marivan. (Credit: Kameel Ahmady)

Article 24 of the CRC emphasizes the minor's health which FGM would violate if carried out in childhood, as it generally is.

Ms. Shirin Talandeh, a lawyer from the Island of Qeshm whose FGM rate exceeds all others in Iran, confirms:

The Iranian penal system features broad and general provisions that prohibit bodily mutilation. According to article 479 of the Islamic penal code passed in 1991 with articles 663 and 664 appended in 2013, female genital mutilation is punishable by the payment of blood money. According to article 12 of the Iranian Constitution, it seems that the legislator's purpose was enactment of a general rule. Now, Islam (specifically the Jaafari school of Islamic jurisprudence) is the official state religion although the followers of other branches of the faith (such

Photo 21. Women discussing FGM in Kermanshah.
(Credit: Kameel Ahmady)

as Hanafi, Shafi'i, Maliki, Hanbali and Zaydi) are free to adhere to their own religious ceremonies and obligations. In other words, if FGM were considered a religious duty, no female victim would be able to claim compensation in court. However, according to article 21, paragraph 1 of the Constitution, the government must ensure the rights of women in all respects. The overall picture is thus a somewhat confusing one, and the Iranian civil code does not help as it does not address FGM.[16]

Attorney-at-law Mr. Mansour Eskandari in Tehran interprets further. He believes that, according to the Iranian penal code, FGM victims "might seek redress [by appealing to] the Law on the Protection of the Rights of Children and Adolescents passed in 2003." Article 1 paragraph 4 states: "Any intentional abuse of children that ignores their mental and physical health or forces them to leave school is prohibited, and the wrongdoer could be sentenced to three to six months' imprisonment or fined 10,000,000 Rials." Still, because article 5 classifies child abuse as a criminal offence, "the [very] need for a civil complaint in FGM cases" is moot.

To understand what might be possible under these provisions, let's apply the prism of Sharia constraints to FGM. Under Sharia, time is of the essence: if excision were necessary, cutting would have to proceed when it is practical, i.e. in infancy; delay means it must be prevented, a prohibition that does not violate any Islamic obligations.

Thus, although Islamic jurisprudence does not criminalize female genital mutilation, the affected person could file a lawsuit using articles 21, 22 and 34 of the Iranian Constitution. And article 3 of the civil code ensures that judges would hear the

---

[16] For further detail, go to http://mb-soft.com/believe/txw/jafari.htm Accessed 8 February 2016.

case. Refusal on the pretext of silent rules, vague statutes, conflict among or excessively broad regulations would not stand up in court.

One question springs to mind, however. Who can sue on behalf of victimized minors? As we have seen, article 5 of the Law on the Protection of the Rights of Children and Adolescents grants the attorney general tools to pursue cases. Additionally, according to article 66 of the criminal law passed in 2014, "NGOs whose statutes explicitly list among their duties protection of children, adolescents and women can file lawsuits against offenders." Furthermore, note 2 of the same criminal code obliges judicial authorities to inform victims that such charities exist. In the final analysis, we might inquire whether parents have the right to put their offspring through the torment of genital cutting. The answer is "no"; both Sharia and parental responsibility laws make clear that parents are guardians who do not "own" their child. To illustrate, article 158 of the Islamic penal code stipulates: "The actions of ... parents and guardians of children to protect and discipline them are not punishable, but the same actions are punishable if the person in question would no longer belong to the category 'child'."

Clearly, sturdier laws can reduce FGM – if only slightly. Legislation alone is insufficient to eradicate it. Securing this aim entails long-term engagement on the part of communities themselves, particularly influential elites, clerics, *bibis* and law enforcement working together with regional and central governments.

Major Contributing Factors

Ending FGM therefore requires joint effort by activists and the injured. But who is involved? According to Salam and De

Waal, "Countries successful in reducing the [incidence] of FGM … have used varied methods: sponsoring alternative rites of passage …, campaigning for rejection of the custom [by] both brides and grooms, engaging clerics and prescribing certain concrete actions."

One hypothesis concerning the custom's origin sees it as a 'practical' measure. Patriarchy had already become firmly entrenched; hence, ensuring women's fidelity and security in fatherhood made control seem essential, especially if men should absent themselves for a considerable time. Salam and De Waal link this to the social acceptance of women by their communities and societies (Salam and De Waal, 2001) – a courteous way of implying that women's nonconformity would otherwise entail harassment.

Photo 22. Wedding in Hawraman, Kurdistan.
(Credit: Kameel Ahmady)

The following passages provide an overview of the role played by the group and other stakeholders in maintaining FGM.

Often it is governments that violate the human rights of citizens. Conversely, implementing many human rights is impossible in the absence of state support. Often, however, patriarchal norms prevail even when a regime attempts to guarantee protection, especially concerning women and children – as the flaunting of legislation in Egypt and tenacity of cutting in Iran show, despite fatwas denying the Islamic status of the cut. Not patriarchy alone but also political structures and systems are responsible for this.

Another obstacle to abolition is the fact that most genital ablations are performed without any direct involvement of men, and some of them are genuinely ignorant of what occurs (euphemism hides the blood) even though, ironically, it is they who (mainly) pay. In Kurdish and southern areas of Iran, however, most men are at least aware of the practice.

This "disconnect" seems to apply to other "women's issues" as well. To illustrate, studies confirm that significant numbers of men lack knowledge of female reproductive health; in most societies under discussion, anything to do with females' 'private parts' is considered off limits, thus making it 'dishonorable' for men to meddle with a 'secret' practice. Yet these same men who would prefer to disengage can be influenced by clerics and imams who preach about diverse benefits of FGM, confirming a (fictional) link to religion. Hence, changing the content of sermons is essential.

Moreover, attitudes of some survivors are revealing. A good number believe that, in possession of an evil and dangerous organ, an unshorn female cannot be a "full woman." The clitoris must be amputated because the unscathed cannot acquire dignity or preserve their chastity. (Ironically, proponents act in accord with Simone de Beauvoir's mantra: Women are made, not born.) These supporters accept FGM without question, moreover, as an old tradition in a social context that highly values continuity. Finally, performed mainly on children, FGM wounds victims too young to consent. They come around, however. Understanding their pain as mandatory for marriage – a social and economic constraint as well as a life's fulfilment – the girls, now mothers, pass the maiming on.

More on the Male Perspective

Although FGM takes place within a female realm, the role of husbands and brothers cannot be overlooked. Some hide behind religion, labeling any endeavor to end FGM a Western derivative of 'women's lib'. And although they may not acknowledge it, many are aware that the scarred vaginal entrance, tighter due to artificial inelasticity, increases sexual pleasure – for the male. In any case, in most conservative cutting cultures, men refuse to marry an unharmed girl.

Some Iranians are convinced, moreover, that FGM dampens women's sexual drive. Compared with Shia Persian or Turkish groups, they would brag, their community is purer, with fewer moral problems. Often Sunni men would assure us of this. If their women had been spared the blade, they said, they would be like Shia females or TV and film stars -- out of control. Regarding sexual intercourse with intact partners from elsewhere in Iran, the smoother and smaller 'circumcised' genitalia, better for sex, were often preferred despite uncut women's advantage at foreplay.

Finally, FGM was unknown to a number of respondents who were equally ignorant of their own wives' genital status. Interestingly, once we outlined the dangers and impairment of women's erotic potential – i.e. that the cut partner's delayed arousal might impede men's marital amusement –, most confirmed that, indeed, sexual relations at home could be improved. Some admitted that their women were "not hot" or "do not give us pleasure." They also confessed that to stoke their own desire, they had other lovers or simply indulged in a younger second wife. And when, later, they were asked whether, in light of their new knowledge, they would be willing to have their daughters cut, exposing them to the same agony in bed and perhaps to a husband who cheats, these men could not answer. Instead, silent, they looked away.

Religion: For or Against FGM?

Here I introduce the four Sunni Islamic schools of jurisprudence and their views on 'circumcision'.

Hanafi and Maliki schools: 'Circumcision' inheres in human nature but is not obligatory. It is recommended for men. For women, in contrast, although better when practiced, it is not recommended (Ibn Aabedin, Ibn Jazee, Albaahi, Ibn Al-jalaab).

Hanbali School: 'Circumcision' is unambiguous regarding men. For them, it is obligatory. For women, however, two hadiths contradict each other. The stronger recommends it but the other calls it obligatory for women as well as men (Ibn Ghedameh, Ibn Teemeeye, Almardawee).

Shafi'i school: As with the Hanbali School, men must undergo circumcision but again, for women, two hadiths guide behavior. The more authentic verse implies obligation to 'circumcise' females. The second which was weak when issued is confirmed by most Shafi'i scholars today. It recommends cutting girls.

The procedure is described in the hadith that requires female 'circumcision'. Amputation targets only a snippet of the clitoris, the removal of flesh considered symbolic or minimal and not as mutilating the organ. The saying concludes with corresponding advice: The less you cut the clitoris, the better. For clarity, this hadith opens with the term *qila* that implies a weak statement. It has been confirmed, however, and recited by most scholars so that over time it has come to be regarded as stronger ("Tohfeh" Abn Alnhaj. Volume 9. p. 198-199).

Why are these details important? Innumerable activists insist that FGM is not in the *Qur'an* and that no religion requires it. Yet the truth is, in Iran and many Muslim countries, cutting girls' genitalia is justified mainly by religious arguments. A campaign to challenge FGM by an NGO in Sudan in 1998 faced strong opposition from Islamic clerics who advised the Muslim community to resist Western pressure and stick to traditional norms. Similarly, imams in Iraqi Kurdistan's Sulaimaniyah label 'ignorant' those who believe that female 'circumcision' is not an Islamic practice.

It is worth stressing that most Muslims do not practice or even know about FGM. This may explain the silence from the non-Shafi'i world even after broad media coverage and international interest dramatically elevated public awareness.

Photo 23. Hormuz Island. (Credit: Kameel Ahmady)

I insist, however, that FGM is indeed *not* an Islamic obligation; genital cutting conflicts with numerous aspects of Islam. Nonetheless, an ordinary person's limited acquaintance with theology might lead him or her to relate it to the faith, while strict Shafi'i Muslims fervently espouse male and 'female circumcision'.

Again I emphasize, FGM is not a constituent aspect of Islam. During the time of the Prophet Muhammad, its practice had been anchored for millennia in the habits of many tribal groups. As Sara Ali in her book *A Woman under Threat* confirms: "The *Qur'an*, a text providing mainly general guidelines (with some injunctions or laws spelled out specifically), does not address ... circumcision of either males or females. The *Qur'an* does, however, refer to the sexual relationship in marriage as one of mutual satisfaction that is considered a mercy from Allah" (Hassan, 1990).

The *Qur'an* clearly promotes mutual pleasure between a husband and wife: "It is lawful for you to go in unto your wives during the night preceding the (day's) fast: they are as a garment for you and you are as a garment for them" (2:187). Moreover: "And of His signs is that He created for you from yourselves mates that you may find tranquility in them; and He placed between you affection and mercy" (30:21). Logically, then, any act that interferes with a gratifying sexual relationship contradicts the essence of Islam. *Fiqah Alnajai*, a book of jurisprudence, echoes this: "The power of men and women to have sexual intercourse and take pleasure from it is a gift [of] God to human beings. This power is one of the strongest instinctive abilities in animals. According to Islamic laws, the power to enjoy sexual intercourse is [a distinct] goal. Therefore, it belongs to the basic rights of every human being."[17]

---

[17] Fiqh Alnjai V3 P 395 Dr. Mustafa Algn, Dr. Mustafa Albga, Dr. Ali Alshbi.

An FGM FAQ published by the UK-based FORWARD (Foundation for Women's Health Research and Development) strengthens our contention that Islam and FGM are fundamentally incompatible. "Although the *Qur'an* mentions many duties regarding women such as pregnancy, breast-feeding, divorce, menstruation, etc., it says nothing about FGM." Rather, scriptures teach that "In God's creation, everything is complete. God does not create anything with fault." FGM can thus be seen as an intrusion that, by deforming God's perfect creation, subjugates women to deprive them of pleasure and their divine rights as human beings.

This interpretation notwithstanding, some people persist in justifying FGM using the sayings (hadith) of the Prophet Muhammad of which we find several interpreted as supporting the cut. One, known as the hadith of 'circumcision', is often told thus:

> Muhammad met a woman called Umme Attiyyah ... known to be a circumciser of female slaves. Muhammad said to her: "Trim, but do not cut into it, for this is brighter for the face and more favorable to the husband."[18]

Now, this ambiguous saying has been used by both supporters and opponents. Backers are greatly relieved to find that FGM is not forbidden; adversaries celebrate the Prophet's advice to keep cutting to a minimum, which in practice they understand to mean doing no harm at all.

The life of Prophet Muhammad serves as a model of Quranic teaching. Since the *Qur'an* does not discuss female 'circumcision', the reliability of this hadith is also suspect, and a compiler of hadiths, Abu Dawud classifies it as "weak." In fact, his is the only one of the six classic hadith collections to contain

---

[18] Sunan Abu Dawûd, Book 41, No. 5251.

Photo 24. Wedding in south of Iran. (Credit: Shirin Talandeh)

it (Chapter 1888). According to Sayyed Sabiq, a renowned scholar and author of *Fiqh-us-Sunnah*, all hadiths concerning female 'circumcision' are inauthentic.

In sum, much debate belabors the issue, and many Muslim scholars have provided evidence both for and against FGM. In 2006, a conference held in Egypt at Al-Azhar University in Cairo, attended by eminent religious scholars, concluded that wounding of girls' vulvas should be banned as it is outside Islam. Professor Ali Goma, then the Grand Mufti of Egypt, viewed clitoridectomy as "punishable aggression against humankind," telling the conference that "female genital circumcision ... harms women psychologically and physically. Therefore, in support of one of the highest values of Islam, namely to do no harm to another – in accordance with the commandment of the Prophet Mohammed 'Accept no harm and do no harm…' the practice must be stopped."[19]

Fatwa on FGM in Kurdish Iraq-English Translation

When asked about Islamic jurisprudence and its own point of view, the Kurdistan High Committee for Fatwa responded: "… In fact Islam did not introduce excision. An old tradition, it is prevalent among antique peoples. The famous classic Greek historian Herodotus says that in ancient times the Egyptians, Assyrians, Kussidiuns and Ethiopians carried it out. Others learned the practice from the Egyptians."[20]

Sheikh Mahmood Shaltot, formerly of Al-Azhar, agrees that FGM is a primordial custom performed since the dawn of history. Thus, it simply continued after the appearance of Islam, and Shaltot's pronouncement, in turn, lead to the fatwa issued in 2010 by the Higher Committee of Fatwa in Iraqi Kurdistan. That body reconfirmed the prior existence of clitoridectomy, thereby corroborating the absence of links to the faith. This gift to abolitionists notwithstanding, the Higher Committee also claimed that FGM is Sunnah so the practice could go unpunished. The fatwa was poorly received by opponents, of course. Whereas the Al-Azhar conference left no room for female genital ablations and provided firm grounds for ending the cutting, the fatwa committee had created a loophole to continue it.

---

[19] http://www.stopfgmmideast.org/fatwas-against-fgm/ Accessed 20 February 2016.

[20] The Higher Committee of Fatwa in Kurdistan, July 6th 2010. Translated from the Kurdish by Goran Sabir. http://www.taskforcefgm.de/en/2010/07/irak-fatwa-genitalverstuemmelung-erlaubt/ Accessed 12.04.2016.

توصيـــات المؤتمـر
*****

بسم الله الرحمن الرحيم

انعقد "مؤتمر العلماء العالمي نحو حظر انتهاك جسد المرأة" في الأول والثاني من ذي القعدة ١٤٢٧هـ الموافق ٢٢ – ٢٣/١١/٢٠٠٦م في رحاب الأزهر، وألقي فيه عدد من البحوث، وبعد مناقشات السادة العلماء والأطباء والمتخصصين والمهتمين من مؤسسات المجتمع المدني في مصر وأوربا وأفريقيا توصل المؤتمر إلى ما يلي:

١. كرم الله الإنسان فقال تعالى: ﴿وَلَقَدْ كَرَّمْنَا بَنِي آدَمَ﴾ فحرم الاعتداء عليه أيًّا كان وضعه الاجتماعي، ذكرًا كان أم أنثى.

٢. ختان الإناث عادة قديمة ظهرت في بعض المجتمعات الإنسانية، ومارسها بعض المسلمين في عدة أقطار تقليدًا لهذه العادة دون استناد إلى نص قرآني أو حديث صحيح يحتج به.

٣. الختان الذي يمارس الآن يلحق الضرر بالمرأة جسميًّا ونفسيًّا، ولذا يجب الامتناع عنه امتثالاً لقيمة عليا من قيم الإسلام؛ وهي عدم إلحاق الضرر بالإنسان، كما قال رسول الله صلى الله عليه وسلم "لا ضرر ولا ضرار في الإسلام" بل يُعد عدوانًا يوجب العقاب.

٤. يناشد المؤتمر المسلمين بأن يكفوا عن هذه العادة، تماشيًا مع تعاليم الإسلام التي تحرم إلحاق الأذى بالإنسان بكل صوره وألوانه.

٥. كما يطالبون الهيئات الإقليمية والدولية ببذل الجهد لتثقيف الناس وتعليمهم الأسس الصحية التي يجب أن يلتزموا بها إزاء المرأة، حتى يقلعوا عن هذه العادة السيئة.

٦. يُذكّر المؤتمر المؤسسات التعليمية والإعلامية بأن عليهم واجبًا محتمًا نحو بيان ضرر هذه العادة، والتركيز على آثارها السيئة في المجتمع، وذلك للإسهام في القضاء على هذه العادة.

٧. يطلب المؤتمر من الهيئات التشريعية سن قانون يُحرّم ويُجرّم من يمارس عادة الختان الضارة فاعلاً كان أو متسببًا فيه.

٨. كما يطلب من الهيئات والمؤسسات الدولية مد يد المساعدة بكافة أشكالها إلى الأقطار التي تُمارس فيها هذه العادة كي تعينها على التخلص منها.

Sects and FGM: Religious Complications in Iran

As we have seen, the Shia-led Iranian government is reluctant to intervene against FGM because it is considered a Sunni Shafi'i practice found mainly in underdeveloped Kurdish border provinces and among Sunni Persian-speaking communities in the south. After all, sectarian rivalry among Sunnis and Shias is centuries old. A lack of trust on religious and ethnic grounds infects relations between the two branches, so any 'high-handed' intervention by the state might spark feelings of resentment.

For this study, in addition to lobbying Sunni religious leaders in FGM-affected areas, we visited the holy cities of Qom and Mashhad where most of the 18 *Marja-i-Taqlid*[21] maintain official advisory offices. They hold what are called Knowledge Rings *(Helqei Mahreft)* two days each week. Some of these Grand Ayatollahs were consulted, either in person or via their representatives, about the validity of FGM within Shia Islam. Although a few responses were mutually contradictory, these men stressed that FGM is more firmly rooted in Sunni Islam and not obligatory for Shias. If found among Shia minorities in parts of Iran or Iraq, the reason lies in the proximity to a mainly Sunni population and is more cross-cultural than anything else.

Shia fatwas, of course, won't carry much weight amongst the Sunni population anyway. Sunni Muslims, moreover, mainly follow 'Sunna', i.e. tradition – which implies that accepting fatwas as guides to behavior is not as common as it is among Shias.

Now, the above discussion reveals a dilemma, that fatwas issued by clerics of the Shia sect such as *Marja-i-Taqlid* would

---

[21] Marja or Source of Emulation are Shia authorities who make legal decisions based on Islamic law. Out of 25 Shia Marja-i-Taqlid, eighteen live in Iran.

Photo 25. Clergy opposing FGM in Gamberon Village, Hormozgan (Credit: Kameel Ahmady)

likely influence Sunni FGM supporters only weakly if at all. Moreover, any attempt to impose Shia fatwas could backfire, igniting anger among Sunnis. Though Shias comprise the ruling power in Iran, for parliamentary purposes, support of Sunni clerics can smooth approval of new legislation. Hence, irritating desired allies is avoided.

Figure 43. Malahasan Vazhi. (Credit: www.facebook.com/malahasan.vazhi?fref=pb&hc_location=friends¬_tab&pnref=friends.all)

Perspectives of Prominent Clerics

Our research unncovered 14 different fatwas, guiding notes and recommendations from Iranian Sunni clerics and made useful contacts with prominent clergy and officials within the Sunni Clerics Council of Kurdistan, West Azerbaijan, Kermanshah and Hormozgan provinces. Some of them condemned FGM. However, fatwas issued in one province may not exert influence in another nor, in some cases, even in nearby villages. Given that each little town has its mosque and independent holy men whose salary is paid by local contributions, any fatwa that clergy of the same rank issue, even right next door, may be dismissed as weak or invalid by the municipal religious authority.

Some Sunni clerics' views are offered here. In general, they either approved the idea of abandoning FGM or supported the practice. Viewpoints of both camps are featured in the short documentary *In the Name of Tradition.*

Mullah Talib Mudizadeh from Bandar Pahl, Hormozgan province, wrote in 2010:

> Regarding the proven medical and psychological dangers of female circumcision and concrete accounts testifying that it causes frigidity and sexual problems in marriage; also considering that religion always puts great emphasis on science and that the Prophet of Islam has said, "Go in quest of science, even to China," and most sciences have proven the disadvantages of this act, insisting that it shouldn't be performed, so it is better not do it. My wife (Mulavi Amineh) and I have always

Photo 26. Dar Al Ahsan Mosque in Mahabad, West Azerbaijan province. (Credit: Kameel Ahmady)

strongly recommended to people of this port and neighboring villages not to circumcise their daughters even if circumcision is good and compulsory for their sons. (Bandar Pahl, Hormozgan, December 2010).

Mulavi Sheikh Salahedin Charaki from Parsian, Hormozgan province, 2012, has written:

There are solid reasons why female circumcision is no longer needed. It has many disadvantages and can lead to men's disloyalty if husbands take several wives. Imam Shafi'i entertains two different opinions about circumcision while other Sunni imams do not believe it is com-

Photo 27. Pupils studying religion in Hormozgan. (Credit: Shirin Talandeh)

pulsory. Therefore, I think now that it has been proven not good for sexual relations, and [since] the extent of cutting remains undefined, not doing it would be better and more appropriate. I have not circumcised any of my three daughters because I fear the risks to their body and soul. (Parsian, Hormozgan province, April 2012).

The most interesting and nuanced but equivocal point of view came from Hajji Mullah Seyyed Hassan Vazhi, Sunni cleric from Piranshar in West Azerbaijan province. Aware that new medical knowledge stresses how female 'circumcision' ravages body and mind, he nonetheless references the Imam Shafi'i and the hadith already cited which calls girls' 'circumcision' good for brightening the face, increasing sexual appetite and easing intercourse for women. With this is mind, he argues that we cannot immediately rule out FGM, but according to the general inference from Islam about injuring anyone by an act or acts; the fact that medical science now considers female 'circumcision' harmful; and the general advice to cut only a little, Islam gives authority to decide whether or not to be cut to the girl herself. "She can seek the opinion of a specialist and in case of availability of an expert circumciser, after reaching a legal age, can make the decision to do it or not," he says, and continues, "Parents are not required to have their children circumcised; the decision rests with the sons and daughters. In case parents are doubtful or insist on circumcision, Shafi'i adherents can follow the principles of three other schools of Sunni jurisprudence, which do not make female circumcision compulsory. For Sunnis, under certain circumstances, switching from their usual school is allowed." Moreover, he goes on, "in my opinion, girls' circumcision provides no benefits, and I have personally warned my family members, relatives and friends against it. I also mention female circumcision in my sermons during Friday prayers and have prevented it in my family" (Ashara al-Mubasharîn Mosque, Piranshar, West Azerbaijan, April 2015).

Similarly, Elham Mondegari, in her thesis *Violation of Women's Bodily Integrity from a Human Rights Perspective*, reports the views of two Sunni clerics in the south of Iran. Sheikh Ahmad Rahmani holds that "fallibility exists in all religions. If it was not so, Imam Shafi'i himself would not have two opinions, [that] cutting the sexual organs of women [is] both *wajib* (compulsory) and *mustahabb* (recommended). What might be the sources of error? Perhaps Imam Shafi'i has old and new sayings, the old belonging to time spent in Iraq when his masters' opinions or available hadiths may have influenced him. Once in Egypt, where surely he met other scholars, on some issues he may have revised his views."

In contrast, Qeshm Island's Sheikh Mohammad Mehdi states:
Not all sages agree regarding the tenets of religion. If, when FGM was compulsory, theology reigned supreme in its own realm, nowadays, on certain issues, many of Imam Shafi's fatwas no longer pertain. Indeed, we have gotten to the point where some hadiths, in certain venues, may be inapplicable because they are *Ejtehaadi* (interpretative). This is the case with circumcision. What I mean is that a number of edicts issued by the Shafi'i School are germane only in Egypt. Not unlike previous eras ... Imam Shafi's fatwas may have been broadly appropriate and yet inapplicable in Iran. ... What is compulsory in one place may be useless somewhere else (Interview with the author. Translated from the Farsi. Bandar Kong, April 2012).

Elham Mondegari also interviewed Mullah Jamal Aldin Vazhi in Pesve, a village in West Azerbaijan province. Drawing on research and pastoral counseling, – not 'gossip' –, he attributes many cases of adultery in Pesve to lack of mutual satisfaction in sexual relations. Each partner blames the other and subsequently seeks pleasure from a third party, a behavior, the Mullah argues, that is rooted in non-Islamic female 'circumcision'. Furthermore, he has uncovered gynecologists' suggestions that in some cases hypertrophied labia minora disturb the marriage bed. Extrapolating from medical texts, he therefore holds that only a minute part of the vulva may be grazed. A word of caution is in order here, however. At the time of this study, no reports had been published linking a large clitoris or hypertrophied labia minora to disturbances in marital relations in Iran.

In sum, changing ordinary perceptions of FGM is closely linked to altering clerics' beliefs. Criticism has compelled prominent Islamic scholars to research the *Quran* and hadiths and has brought some positive pronouncements against clitoridectomy. Some high-profile sheikhs and faith leaders, including several brave Iranian Sunni spokesmen, have denounced genital ablation in clear terms or called it "permissible but not obligatory." The earlier quotes give an idea of the range of arguments deployed.

Thus it appears that four schools[22] of Islamic jurisprudence consider it obligatory or preferable although some scholars from Al-Azhar University in Cairo have their own stance which contradicts that of these four schools.

---

[22] Shafi'i, Hanafi, Maliki, Hanabli.

Legal Retribution or Compensation for FGM

As we have seen, pro-FGM clerics in Iranian Kurdistan and the South of Iran require 'female circumcision'. They base their arguments on the hadith mentioned earlier which can be interpreted as limiting the intervention to a minor cut. Many forms of FGM are viewed, however, as extreme and injurious from every perspective – for example, amputation of the labia.

Islamic jurists from all four schools state that cutting both vaginal lips can justify the sufferer's demanding reparations of full *diyya;* and if only one is shorn, then a half *diyya*.[23] The idea is that loss of ability to enjoy sexual intercourse should entail the greatest amount of financial compensation *(diyya)* equal to the sum awarded for murder (blood money). For example, if someone breaks another's spine, the victim deserves one full *diyya* for the resulting paralysis and another for losing the ability to have sex. And when a man is wounded, if he can manage erections but not ejaculation or orgasm, this rule applies.[24]

Furthermore, "Tohfeh," one of Shafi's canonical sources, states that injured males even when able to have intercourse but unable to derive pleasure from it must receive full *diyya*. Applying the same ruling to women, we can argue that 'Pharaonic circumcision', i.e. infibulation, entitles the girl to full *diyya*.[25]

Given that certain clerics see female 'circumcision' as a religious rite and therefore not a crime, no specific discussion is devoted to it in exegeses on *diyya* or wrongdoing. Yet another general principle states that if no specific compensation is defined for abuse or harm, the judicial system must determine it.

---

[23] Mgna Almtaj Shrbini V4 P 74 & Nahaite Almetleb, Jotini V 16 P 437.

[24] Tohfeh Almtaj Aben Hejer V8 P 482 & Nahaite Almetleb, Jotini V 16 P 437.

[25] Tohfeh, V 8 P 482.

Thus, considering the importance of erotic satisfaction, the court fixes the extent of damage and corresponding *diyya*. That is, loss of jouissance is included in cases for which full *diyya* should be paid.[26] Circumcisers can therefore be liable under Islam if, while cutting, they fail to follow to the letter instructions to remove little flesh, thereby inflicting serious injury on sexual organs and becoming obliged to pay full *diyya*.[27]

Needless to say, this conclusion is less than welcome to proponents of total abolition.

---

[26] Megni Almtaj V4 P 77 & Tohfeh V8 P 482.
[27] Beihaqi V8 P 325.

CHAPTER FOUR

Conclusions, Lessons & Recommendations

Worldwide, FGM occurs to subjugate females in the name of culture and belief. Though not imposed by any creed, communities link Islam to the procedure in order to compel compliance. Religious preferences for 'purity' and 'chastity' justify genital ablation. By this reasoning, women's desires ought to be suppressed. And most challenging of all, women who idealize virginity perpetuate the practice.

As to geographical dispersion, Africa is its heartland followed by the Middle East and Asia, yet Diaspora has ensured excision's global spread. As migrants make new lives elsewhere, the custom moves with them. Australia, New Zealand, Canada, Europe, and the United States are now dealing with this imported healthcare crisis (Wood, 2001; WHO, 2008; Malmström et al., 2011).

For UNICEF data show massive numbers suffering sequelae of genital ablation and, as a result, presenting to mainly unprepared and uninformed gynecologists and obstetric units. Now that figures from Indonesia are in, estimates have reached 200 million mutilated, with 3 million girls each year living in fear of cutting. Although in some countries, the practice is slowly receding, monitoring is deficient, making assessment of past campaigns difficult. We can draw general conclusions, nonetheless, to strengthen interventions.

In chapter 1 we dealt with global prevalence and the historical background of FGM as a hoary patriarchal tradition. The bond between ablation and religion was also queried, since excision predates both Christianity and Islam; some Christians excise in Eritrea and Jews, for instance, in Ethiopia, presented evidence of genital wounds when examined in Israel upon moving there. But the rite is not limited to monotheists: communities with animist and other traditional beliefs, such as Aboriginal Australians, also mutilate the genitals.

Chapter 2 dealt with the prevalence of FGM in Iran where clitoridectomy plays a profound role in social and cultural power structures, suggesting that the custom's resilience requires work against it to be both comprehensive and protracted. Preliminary data illuminate connections among prevalence, motives and culture, inspiring campaign design.

The data also indicate, however, that in certain nations and among ethnicities where interventions have been on-going,

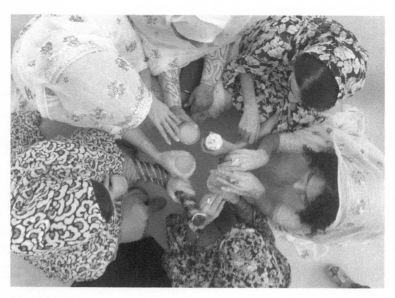

Photo 28. Engagement ceremony, south of Iran.
(Credit: Shirin Talandeh)

sometimes for two decades, prevalence remains unchanged. Why? The question is hard to answer, given the dearth of professional evaluation. Findings should thus be reviewed in light of defenses that underpin the practice.

One such defense takes the form of silence, a suppression of information that impedes the emergence of data. FGM, therefore, has been (almost) invisible; government, in any case, has been reluctant to admit its existence and civil society, too, keeps it under wraps. In some quarters, the subject remains taboo.

Our study, therefore, highlights research extracted at risk and presented mainly in non-local female scholars' postgraduate theses.

Photo 29. Women asked about FGM, Kuzestan province.
(Credit: Shirin Talandeh)

Photo 30. Children in southern Iran. (Credit: Shirin Talandeh)

Data clearly show the highest rates of FGM in Hormozgan province, although it is also common in the north-west and west of Iran.

In chapter 3 we looked at the roles of national and international treaties and domestic jurisprudence in efforts to eradicate the practice. Although 'female circumcision' is not imposed by Islam, clerics and imams play a significant role in perpetuating it. Our research also strongly suggests that laws alone cannot change perceptions; needed is a firm commitment on the part of communities and government working together to eradicate it.

Lessons Learned from the Research and Pilot Program

Our ten-year study tour taught us a lot. The work benefitted from engaging with communities at all levels, and the groups with whom we sought interaction participated. The research has provided government and human rights organizations with new information about the ills attendant upon FGM and how genital cutting infringes human rights. This in turn has replaced silence with awareness. However modest, a paradigm shift towards ending the practice has emerged.

Benefitting from consistent recalibration based on our discoveries, the pilot interventions gradually transitioned from providing medical care to teaching about FGM by lobbying and networking with stakeholders, religious figures and the community.

Photo 31. Wedding in Qeshm, Hormozgan.
(Credit: Shirin Talandeh)

A caveat exists, however. Although education and advocacy demonstrated the aptness of our 'toolkit' to illuminate hidden facts, new knowledge proved insufficient to eliminate FGM, at heart an emotional issue. Similarly, concentrating on health hazards appears to have encouraged modified patterns of cutting. Nonetheless, combining awareness-raising with unequivocal opposition to medicalization has decreased the number of cut girls. Beyond that, further intervention ought to explore alternative yet harmless initiation rites for daughters.

Our research also revealed that any enduring, productive effort must cultivate the trust of local and national government. To address FGM, the best mediation partners are the UN and the UNFPA present in Tehran with whom the health ministry and social services already negotiate and in whom they apparently have confidence. Future cooperation among such agencies is vital to transfer experience and data, and NGOs rely on them to appeal to the regime on their behalf.

Community ownership and integrated socioeconomic development are among the most promising approaches. Indeed, all social groups, including health workers, prominent religious, civic leaders and local authorities have a role to play in opposing FGM. A holistic concern considers people's basic needs while at the same time focusing on rights and health-related issues. In addition, communities' ability to promote change and to empower themselves internally should be fortified. Although the pilot interventions found it challenging to involve religious figures, winning them over proved essential, especially for those who insist that FGM is intrinsic to Islam.

On a more subjective note, an unobtrusive observation concerns the self-reinforcing behavior of mothers in FGM-practicing areas. The tradition's tenacity lodges in the home where mothers organize a new round of brutality. Despite (or because of?) their experience, they transfer the legacy of pain and torment to the next generation. Of course, for them, the motivating factor is the good life they believe their daughters will enjoy after 'circumcision', because mutilation guarantees marriage. Ultimately, social consensus under patriarchy must cede to the realization that subjugating women by controlling their sexuality is an unjustified and harmful, not to mention fruitless act.

The Way Forward: Recommendations

The following recommendations, inspired by the findings of a decade-long, challenging journey, reflect not only the researchers' views but, more important, those of the communities and other stakeholders involved.

- The significance of government in combatting FGM cannot be over-emphasized. The regime's understanding of 'circumcision' as a violation of rights would encourage the community to view excision not only as a threatening and morally bankrupt practice but also as one that is not legally sound. Once Tehran acknowledges the existence of this abuse and embraces a rights-based approach, developing an effective action plan should be the next step, one synchronized with universal human rights commitments. The regime should facilitate ending this danger to public health by demonstrating accountability, providing supervision to national and international organizations, and collaborating with other countries where FGM exists but is in decline.

- Government must merge measures to fight FGM into existing national education and health programs. Equally imperative is ratification of appropriate existing international human rights pacts such as the Women's Convention

Photo 32. Pilot intervention, Kermanshah.
(Credit: Kameel Ahmady)

(CEDAW); the Children's Rights Convention; the International Covenant on Civil and Political Rights; the International Covenant on Economic, Social, and Cultural Rights as well as the Banjul Charter plus European and American Conventions (Rahman and Toubia, 2000). Once these treaties are approved, national legislation can be overhauled to harmonize with them. The aim is, of course, to move as rapidly as possible towards ending FGM in Iran.

- Tehran must also legislate against FGM. Merging community efforts with national exertions can bring a sustained end to the custom. State actors' financial and ideal endorsement of community endeavors will strengthen local advocates,

Photo 33. Woman in typical attire and face covering.
(Credit: Kameel Ahmady)

particularly if Tehran attends to the four affected provinces of Hormozgan, West Azerbaijan, Kermanshah, and Kurdistan. A special action plan should involve provincial ministries of the respective provinces and authorities.

- National health, social services and the education ministry should resource rural areas with limited or no access to cities. Healthcare should treat women and girls for FGM-related conditions; national health should train and provide alternative employment for *bibis*. Social services, using mobile teams, could organize meetings, hold face-to-face sessions with affected communities and raise awareness among clerics. The education sector should access nurseries and schools, providing children with wellness-related information and identifying girls who already live with FGM.

- Even if legislation were enacted or existing laws applied, implementation would require immense courage in the Kurdish regions and the south where clerics and influential citizens support the practice in the name of religion and culture. Faith leaders are among the most tenacious in perpetuating FGM, so they must be persuaded to publicly oppose it. In this regard, the pilot intervention has provided a platform for prominent religious to speak out against the ritual. These interventions must become a formal campaign, their sequel ensured through advocacy with and lobbying of clerics to elicit a clear statement denying any religious basis for FGM.

- Developing clinicians' skills is also imperative so that they can reach out to women too timid to come forward with side- and after-effects of FGM. Because health problems related to excision are embarrassing, victims tend to conceal them, making it difficult for doctors to diagnose and provide appropriate care. We need a trained cadre of medical professionals who can identify problems, offer counselling and recommend treatment. Fortunately, this issue has been successfully addressed by our mobile health service in pilot interventions that merit replication and funding. Finally, government must also enhance national reproductive health strategies to address women who have suffered genital mutilation.

- Women and girls whose clitoris has been damaged are also more prone to psychological disturbance than those who have not been 'cut', and the severity depends on multiple

Photo 34. Shia cleric in Holy City of Mashhad.
(Credit: Kameel Ahmady)

factors such as gravity of the incision, cultural context, etc. The trauma must be acknowledged and treated. As mentioned, government recognition of FGM as a women's rights violation would address these concerns. Innovative courses should enable clinicians, counsellors and youth workers to understand the gravity of the intervention and train them to tackle the mental health consequences of genital torture in a diplomatic manner.

- As noted earlier, reconstructive surgery can reverse some effects of FGM (Foldes et al., 2012). This study recommends that government take appropriate measures to introduce such treatments in Iran. They should be covered by national medical insurance to ease access to surgery for poor and vulnerable women.

- Sympathetic local media can have a profound effect on the context of FGM. Our pilot interventions privileged journalism as an avenue to curb the cutting. Media coverage of community efforts is helpful, including online interviews with clerics and medical professionals about the ill effects of the practice.

- After preparing the ground, a trained cadre of youngsters is required for effective dialogue using social networking. Traditional print media should also be encouraged to cover FGM, supported by government's assurance to writers of freedom to treat the topic without fear of backlash. Media write-ups favoring abolition are essential to hasten the custom's demise with the proviso that capacity-building is offered within the media itself to ensure cultural sensitivity in coverage.

- Education officials should tailor programs for schools in FGM-affected provinces, taking into account local sensitivities.

- So far, Iran lacks a comprehensive national research program to track FGM. Financing is imperative to promote urgently needed competence in monitoring and evaluation. Because resource mobilization can contribute to a sustainable paradigm shift in social norms, organizations and individuals already acting toward this end must be strengthened. NGOs must further be encouraged to demand evidence-based research, and funded academic studies that provide it should also adopt a gender and human rights perspective. A nationwide report on FGM produced with the involvement of healthcare and social services can highlight – and ultimately curb – the cutting.

- In addition to enacting and enforcing legislation, we recommend a participatory approach in affected areas. Guided by courtesy, interventions that address women and girls who have already endured FGM should include key community influencers, most of whom are men, and sustain community-based efforts to change social norms (de Souza and Communication, 2007). Clearly, young female activists' involvement will be helpful in preventing a rite in which women are both perpetrators and victims.

- Agents of change with impact on the local level, NGOs and community-based organizations (CBOs) should enjoy the opportunity to increase their skills. International funding for village groups is needed, and government should discuss this with UN agencies. The Iran-based arms of

UNICEF and UNFPA can empower indigenous associations by sharing their extensive expertise. After all, the UN works to eliminate the practice in most affected nations.

- Difficulties in ending FGM in Iran arise because the Shia branch of Islam is the state religion whereas cutting pertains almost exclusively to Sunnis, and government often lacks community trust in Sunni majority regions. Every civil society organization and NGO reports directly to the capital with suggestions and recommendations, making the regime absolutely crucial. But distrust poses a massive hurdle in campaigns against the practice, implying that local actors and political bodies have a duty to address their differences and work together. Only when Tehran wins the confidence of Sunnis can national efforts to end FGM gain traction and spare little girls the blade.

References

https://www.youtube.com/watch?v=RID4FnKf7oE&feature=youtu.be&noredirect=1 [Online].

Adeniran, A. I. 2008. Educational inequalities and women's disempowerment in Nigeria. *Gender and Behaviour,* 6, 1559-1576.

Ahmady, K. 2006. *FGM in Iran* [Excepts Online]. Available http://kameelahmady.com/ 2015.

Al-Khulaidi, G. A., Nakamura, K., Seino, K. & Kizuki, M. 2013. Decline of supportive attitudes among husbands toward female genital mutilation and its association to those practices in Yemen. *PloS one,* 8, e83140.

Alawi, I. & Schwartz, S. 2015. Female Genital Mutilation a Growing Problem in Iran. http://www.weeklystandard.com/blogs/female-genital-mutilation-growing-problem-iran_824155.html?page=1 Accessed 18 April 2015.

Alsibiani, S. A. & Rouzi, A. A. 2010. Sexual function in women with female genital mutilation. *Fertility and sterility,* 93, 722-724.

Bamberger, M. 2000. *Integrating quantitative and qualitative research in development projects.* World Bank Publications.

Boyle, E. H. & Preves, S. E. 2000. National politics as international process: the case of anti-female-genital-cutting laws. *Law and Society Review,* 703-737.

Brown, I. B. 1866. *On the curability of certain forms of insanity, epilepsy, catalepsy, and hysteria in females.* London: Robert Hardwicke.

de Souza, R. T. & Communication, P. U. 2007. *NGOs and Empowerment: Creating Communicative Spaces in the Realm of HIV/AIDS in India.* Purdue University.

EndFGM European campaign, Amnesty International. https://www.amnesty.org/en/latest/news/2012/11/fight-against-female-genital-mutilation-wins-un-backing/ Accessed 12 April 2016.

"Fatwa on FGM in Kurdish Iraq." http://www.taskforcefgm.de/en/2010/07/irak-fatwa-genital-verstuemmelung-erlaubt/ Accessed 12 April 2016.

Foldès, P., Cuzin, B. & Andro, A. 2012. Reconstructive surgery after female genital mutilation: a prospective cohort study. *The Lancet,* 380, 134-141.

Hassan, R. 1990. An Islamic Perspective. In Becker J., *Women Religion and Sexuality, Studies in the Impact of Religious Teachings on Women.* Geneva: WLC Publications, 93-128.

Hassanian, F. 2012. *Forbidden Female Genital Mutilation (FGM) in International Documents with Emphasis on Practicing Countries.* Master's Thesis, Azad University of Tehran.

Human Rights Watch, "They Took Me and Told Me Nothing," Female Genital Mutilation in Iraqi Kurdistan. *Human Rights Watch,* 86. 16 June 2010. http://www.refworld.org/docid/4c19d34b2.html Accessed 12 April 2016

Iweulmor, J. & Veney, C. 2006. Preserving a Woman's Genitalia: An Analysis of Female Circumcision/Female Genital Mutilation in Africa. *The Penn State McNair Journal,* 27.

Jalali, R., P. 2007. *Analysis of the Cultural Origins of Violence against Women, Emphasizing Circumcision of Women in Bandar Kong.* Postgraduate Thesis, Islamic Azad University.

Karimi, F. 2010. *Tragedy of the Body*. Tehran, Roshangaran and Women Study Publishing.

Khady with Marie-Therese Cuny. 2010. *Blood Stains. A Child of Africa Reclaims Her Human Rights*. Trans. Tobe Levin. UnCUT/VOICES Press.

Lightfoot-Klein, H. 1983. Pharaonic circumcision of females in the Sudan. *Medicine and law*, 2, 353.

Malmström, M., Moneti, F., Donahue, C., Toure, A. & Haug, W. 2011. *UNFPA-UNICEF Joint Programme on Female Genital Mutilation-Cutting: Accelerating Change. Annual Report 2010. Nurturing Change from Within*.

Mandegari, E. 2008. *Violation of Women's Bodily Integrity from a Human Rights Point of View*. Postgraduate Thesis, Shahid Beheshti University.

May, T. 2011. *Social research: Issues, methods and process*. McGraw-Hill Education (UK).

Mohajer, D. F. 2010. *Female Circumcision: Elegy for a Dream* [Online]. http://www.gozaar.org/english/articles-en/Female-Circumcision-Elegy-for-a-Dream.html Accessed 1 April 2015.

Mozafarian, R. 2011. *A survey on social-cultural factors related to Female Genital Mutilation: A case study of age 15-49 in Qeshm Island, 2011*. Master's Thesis, Shiraz University.

Pandit, E. 2012. UN STUDY SHOWS FEMALE GENITAL MUTILATION/CUTTING ON THE DECLINE IN AFRICA [Online]. http://feministing.com/2012/02/07/un-study-shows-female-genital-mutilationcutting-on-the-decline-in-africa/ Accessed 6 April 2015.

Pashaei, T., Majlessi, F. & Rahimi, A. 2011. Health education Promotion. *Health Promotion Perspectives – An International Journal*, 1, 408.

Rahman, A. & Toubia, N. 2000. *Female genital mutilation: A practical guide to worldwide laws & policies.* Zed Books.

RCW, T. R. C. S. 2014. The Achievement of the Girl Summit. https://thercs.org/news/news-and-blog/the-achievement-of-the-girl-summit/[Accessed 30 April 2015.

Robert, D. L. 1996. *American Women in Mission: A Social History of Their Thought and Practice.* Mercer University Press.

Salam, A. H. A. & De Waal, A. 2001. *The Phoenix State: Civil Society and the Future of Sudan.* Red Sea Press.

UNICEF. 2013. *Female Genital Mutilation/Cutting: A statistical overview and exploration of the dynamics of change.* New York: UNICEF.

---- 2014. UNICEF and Partners Release First-Ever Survey of FGM in Northern Iraq [Online]. http://www.uncef.org/mean/MENA-KAP_Survey_Key_Findings_HCWA_UNICEF_FINAL.pdf   Accessed 12 April 2015.

WHO. 2008. *Eliminating Female Genital Mutilation: An interagency statement – OHCHR, UNAIDS, UNDP, UNECA. UNESCO, UNFPA, UNHCR, UNICEF, UNIFEM, WHO, WHO,* Geneva.

Wood, A. N. 2001. Cultural Rite of Passage or a Form of Torture: Female Genital Mutilation from an International Law Perspective. *Hastings Women's Law Journal,* 12, 347.

AfterWords

By Tobe Levin and Hilary Burrage

Is female genital mutilation an African issue? A women's problem? A religious requirement? A feminist concern?

Playing devil's advocate, the answer in every case is that FGM shatters these limiting frames. Ablation of girls' genitalia isn't the unique concern of Africans, women, theologians or feminists. Ending FGM requires all people of good will.

And thanks to Kameel Ahmady and his team's research, the facts are out. Sharp metal objects bite vulvas in Iran, thus providing certainty that FGM exceeds the confines of a continent known to have birthed our earliest recorded ancestor, the woman archaeologists named Lucy. Indeed, these facts imply excision's spread from a Blue Nilotic epicenter to be taken up, for complex reasons, elsewhere around the globe.

Moreover, Kameel Ahmady is a man whose questioning of male peers reveals degrees of men's involvement, broadening ownership and thus accountability beyond the female sphere. Regarding religion, Ahmady opens the door to Farsi discussions inaccessible to most readers of this book, and what he shows is a fascinating potpourri of clerical back and forth. Writ large in most analyses of genital excision is the custom's absence from the Koran and indeed from the scriptures of most faiths. Yet we find the local mullahs differing as to the duties of their flocks. Some tell the devout that releasing clitoral blood is not forbidden; others recommend it; still others leave the decision to the grown-up children; many also counsel against it. Ahmady himself is sure: Islam doesn't condone ablation of a child's genitalia given Koranic commands to 'do no harm'.

And as a feminist issue?

Here, too, Kameel Ahmady stands out among students of these 'rites'. Though in youth he had suspected it, only later in life did he learn of his own female relatives' victimization; empathy with his mother and sisters spurred him to take up the abolition cause. He supports women's empowerment. He understands the challenge to self-confidence resulting from the symbolic and actual infliction of a disability. He sees that clitoral attack, beyond rationalizations and even in the mildest forms that leave few or no physical scars, affects the mind. Why should female organs of sexuality and procreation be handled fiercely rather than gently? What possible psychological reality could account for such behavior as espoused by individuals and groups when the act itself is surely counterintuitive for everyone?

Anthr/apologists have a ready answer: pain itself is valued. If, however, this explanation once sufficed, it does so no longer as human and children's rights have, since at least World War II, presented themselves as universal standards to which Ahmady unequivocally subscribes. Thus, if we define feminism as the theory seeking to enhance the world by cleansing it of gender-based discrimination, FGM is a feminist issue par excellence.

As Verena Stefan writes, "No little girl in the world would, by herself, think up such a thing as placing clitoris and vagina in competition with one another, de- and revaluing them, creating an arbitrary conflict between two parts of her own body or, out of the blue, resolving to amputate a healthy organ."[1] Rather, "the clitoris appears as the primary threat to a phallocratic world view and to the power of individual men."[2]

Ahmady never loses sight of this, reiterating (often) the challenges for him, as a man and a feminist, in trying to stop FGM in Iran. One of his most poignant scenes concerns the colloquy

---

[1] Verena Stefan. (2104) "Mutilation of the Vulva and Circumcision of other Female Freedoms – or the Perfect Vulva's Aura and Revolt." In Levin, Tobe, ed. *Waging Empathy. Alice Walker, Possessing the Secret of Joy and the Global Movement to Ban FGM.* Trans. Tobe Levin. Frankfurt am Main: UnCUT/VOICES P., 69.

[2] Ibid. 68.

of males newly informed of what the custom brings women – risks and pain. "Later [the men] were asked whether, in light of their new knowledge…, they would be willing to have their daughters cut, thereby exposing them to the same agony in bed and perhaps to a husband who cheats. Our interviewees could not answer. Instead," Ahmady writes, "silent, they looked away."

We both agree, Kameel Ahmady's feminist stance is well-defined. The two years of our collaboration, editing his research report to enable publication, have revealed yet again that matters exist unconfined by national or so-called 'cultural' boundaries. We meet men as well as women, in every part of the world, for whom self-determination and bodily integrity are rights everyone should enjoy. As Ahmady has consistently demonstrated in our dialogues in cyberspace, he is one of them. The right to be free from assault and pain, 'even' in the name of tradition, is an entitlement guaranteed to all.

In this belief Ahmady joins an increasing number of men, each applying his particular prism or lens to interpret what he has observed or uncovered. This distinguished cadre of male campaigners against FGM includes activists from many corners of the globe – Morissanda Kouyaté, the Guinean medical doctor who leads the Inter-African Committee in its work; Samuel Leadismo, Evanson Njero, Gerald Lepariyo and Tony Mwebia, all activists in Kenya; the artist Godfrey Williams-Okorodus of Nigeria and Belgium; and advocates Ahmed Hassan and Ahabwe Mugerwa Michael in Somalia and Uganda respectively; Qamar Naseem of the human rights organization Blue Veins in Pakistan; the attorney Dexter Dias QC in the UK; Dr. Pierre Foldes in France; Thomas von der Osten-Sacken of WADI in Iraq, and Holger Postulart, director of the Global Alliance Against FGM based in Geneva.

The net is closing. FGM is being called out and will be defeated by people of different genders, many traditions and creeds, or indeed of no creed at all other than the belief in the universality of human rights.

Beyond the critical significance of these inalienable rights, Kameel Ahmady's focus, like that of his male co-activists identified here, also demonstrates another deep truth: the world over, men as well as women can subscribe sincerely to the feminist ideal. Feminism, they understand, is not about setting women against men; it is about revealing the grim truths of patriarchy, that system which disadvantages many women and some men in the interests of a powerful male minority. Both women and men, they acknowledge, can co-exist more happily and safely when the tools of repression employed to subjugate women are identified and challenged.

Feminism, these thoughtful men understand, is in essence about confronting the abuse of power, and that abuse is exercised, most fundamentally, cruelly and dramatically in the form of genital assault, by some men on many women. No matter that it is women who may execute the actual act; it is performed because the men – often culpably feigning only a vague knowledge of detail – require the erotic taming of the female. In that sense, as Ahmady's work confirms, this 'rite' is, taken literally, patriarchy incarnate, the carving of men's power on and into women's bodies.

The work of unveiling the cutting culture in hitherto unrevealed places, in locations in Iran and elsewhere, is only just beginning, but it could not be more important in the struggle to make FGM history. Kameel Ahmady's contribution to that work is enormous.

Index

Dubai 59

E

Egypt 11, 18, 20, 21, 22, 27, 100 - 102, 108, 115, 116, 124
Ejtehaadi 124
Elham Mandegari 8, 35, 36, 39 - 41, 124, 125
Eritrea 18, 22, 129
Ethiopia 18, 21, 24, 99, 101, 116, 129
European colonial administrators 95
Faculty of Health and Nutrition 40
Fahimeh Hassanian 8, 38, 41
Falasha 24
Fars 31, 50, 51
Farsi 9, 14, 31, 42, 124, 146
Fatimah Karimi 33 - 35
Female Genital Mutilation 7, 10, 11, 16, 19, 37, 40, 41, 42, 98, 99, 104, 105, 146
Feyli 60
FGM, types of 19
Fiqah Alnajai 113
Fiqh-us-Sunnah 115
France 101, 148
Fran Hosken 98

G

Gamberon 119
Garain 59
Gavbandi 58
Gerechi 61
Ghana 98
Gilan 50
Golestan 9, 50, 51
Grand Mufti 115
Guardian Council 102
Gulf region 59

Guinea 100, 148

H
Hadith 111, 114, 115, 123, 124, 125, 126
Haji Mullah Seyyed Hassan Vazhi 8, 123
Hanbali 105, 111
Hanafi 51, 105, 111
Hawaram 42
Hawraman Tekht 60
Helqei Mahreft 118
Herodotus 116
Hittites 21
Hormuz 12, 58, 62, 69 114
Hormozgan 8, 9, 10, 12, 31, 33, 43, 45, 49, 50-53, 57-59, 65, 66, 68, 69, 71-74, 76-80, 82, 85, 87, 90, 119-123, 131, 132, 137
Homa Ahadi 31, 59
Hulda Stumpf 96

I
IAC 98
Ibn Aabedin 111
Ibn Al-jalaab 111
Ibn Ghedameh 111
Ibn Jazee 111
Ibn Teemeeye 111
ICPD 97
Ilam 9, 43, 50, 53
India 21, 44
Indonesia 21, 128
International Congress on Health, Education & Promotion 40
International Conference on Population and Development 97
Iraq 21, 22, 27, 29, 30, 44, 61, 70, 102, 112, 116, 118, 124
Islam 14, 24, 29, 32, 34, 36, 41, 46, 59, 60, 83, 102-106, 111-116,

Laki 60
Larak 62, 63
Liberia 27
Lorestan 50

M

Mahabad 12, 43, 46, 49, 121
Mako 61
Majlessi 40
Malaysia 21
Mali 18, 22
Maliki 105, 111
Mansoor Agai 60
Mansour Eskandari 7, 105
Marja-i-Taqlid 118
Marivan 42, 63
Mauritania 27
Mehran 53
Mehrangiz Kar 43
MICS 56, 64, 66
Miandoab 43
Middle East 16, 20, 21, 29, 30, 101, 102, 128
Minab 31, 58, 59, 84
Minister of Culture and Islamic Guidance 34
Muhammad Khatami 102
Mukriyan 11, 48
Mullah Jamal Aldin Vazhi 125
Mullah Talib Mudizadeh 121
Multiple Indicator Cluster Surveys 56
Muslim 7, 24, 29, 44, 50, 51, 59, 95, 112, 113, 115, 118
Mustahabb 124

N

Nigeria 27, 148

Nodsha 60
Noof 59
Norway 101
Nosod 60

O
Oman 59

P
Paisa Rezazadeh Jalali 33
Pajela 45
Pakistan 7, 21, 148
Parvin Zabihi 8, 42
Pashaei T. 40
Pava 35, 60
Persian 29, 58, 60, 92, 109, 118
Philippines 21
Phoenicians 21
Pilot interventions 11, 14, 74, 92, 132, 133, 138, 139
Pilot program 54, 55, 132
Prophet Muhammad 45, 113, 114

Q
Qeshm Island 12, 40, 44, 49, 58, 62, 69, 72, 84, 90, 104, 124, 144
Qila 111
Qisas 103
Qom 8, 118
Qorveh 59
Quran 24, 36, 93, 114, 125

R
Rahimi A. 40
Ras Al Khaima 59

Each UnCUT/VOICES Press book supports a specific project against FGM. Sales of *In the Name of Tradition. Female Genital Mutilation in Iran* contribute to the **Clitoris Restoration and Fistula Repair Fund** that sponsors operations by Dr. Pierre Foldes and other qualified surgeons at the Institut en Santé Génésique in St. Germain-en-Laye outside Paris, France.

In the United States, your donation is tax deductible. Send a check in any amount made out to **Healthy Tomorrow** with a clear notation that you are contributing to the Clitoris Restoration Fund.
The address: Healthy Tomorrow, 14 William St., Somerville, MA 02144 USA.

You can also make a tax-deductible contribution in Germany by bank transfer to FORWARD – Germany with the clear notation **Clitoris Restoration and Fistula Repair Fund and your email or snail-mail address.**
Transfer to
FORWARD – Germany e.V.
Frankfurter Sparkasse
BLZ 500 502 01
Account # 200029398
IBAN: DE20 5005 0201 0200 0293 98
BIC SWIFT: HELADEF1822

In the UK, an official charity, the Clitoris Restoration and Fistula Repair Fund, is in formation. For information contact the trustees at tobe.levin@uncutvoices.com

Hearty thanks to Steffen Schenk, MaynPrint (Frankfurt, Germany) for generous support with design, lay-out, and production.